CORE STRATEGY FOR SUCCESS

*How to Lead the Pack
in a "Dog-Eat-Dog" World*

Fred A. Manske Jr.

Core Strategy for Success

Published by Leadership Education and Development, Inc.
9 Oxford Drive
Hilton Head Island, SC 29928

Leadership Education Website:
www.leadershipdevelopment.com

Information and book ordering:
leadershipinformation@gmail.com
or 888-325-3987

Although the author and publisher have exhaustively researched all sources to ensure the accuracy and completeness of the information contained in this book, we assume no responsibility for errors, inaccuracies, omissions, or any inconsistencies herein. All slights of people or organizations are unintentional.

Printed in the United States of America
ISBN 978-1-60013-782-2
10 9 8 7 6 5 4 3 2 1

Table of Contents

Table of Contents

Table of Contents

Acknowledgments

Core Strategy for Success would have not been possible without the assistance of a number of people who made content and editing suggestions. They include Lois Claus, Myra and Rebecca Curry, Donna Eberl, Art Gorman, Linda Hatcher, David Lauderdale, and Mel Witmer. But most of all, I'd like to thank my wife, Dr. Donna Manske, who always believed in the book project and provided invaluable input.

Preface

"It is our character that supports the promise of the future."

—William J. Bennett

The book *Core Strategy for Success* challenges readers to reach their highest leadership potential. A person is a leader if he or she is in a position to influence the behavior of people directly or indirectly.

Although the book has a decided business orientation, the values and principles espoused apply equally to all professions and volunteer endeavors where leaders work with others to achieve common objectives.

Core Strategy for Success focuses on the presentation of **three key leadership values.** When a leader consistently operates based on these values, he or she considerably improves the odds of being successful. The core strategy is, in effect, the adoption of the three key values as the primary guide for how one leads. The book provides practical ideas and approaches to help readers implement the strategy.

Core Strategy for Success contains numerous inspiring quotations. From the observations of statesmen, executives, writers, and poets comes a wealth of wisdom that provides understanding, guidance, and inspiration for those aspiring to be a success in life.

The emphasis in the book is on achieving leadership success over the *long run*. Yes, it is possible for selfish, unethical leaders to obtain results for a while. All too often, we've seen this happen. But, seldom do such leaders succeed over the long haul. Eventually their bad deeds are exposed and they fail miserably. Often their careers and personal lives are left in ruins.

With a typical career today spanning more than forty-five years, it makes sense to approach one's career in a manner that leads to long-term success. The primary objective of this book is to help readers in this important quest.

Section One

The "Dog-Eat-Dog" World

Chapter One

The Proliferation of "Dog-Eat-Dog" Attitudes

"All that is necessary for the triumph of evil is that good men do nothing."

—Edmund Burk

In many respects, it appears that we're evolving toward a "dog-eat-dog" world.

According to Peter Buffett, the American composer and author, "We're living in times in which too many people have erroneously decided that their only interest is financial gain and material accumulation." In addition, it seems that telling the truth and being honest are becoming less valued. A recent survey of seven thousand young people conducted by the Josephson Institute of Ethics revealed two significant findings:

1. the majority of teenagers believe that lying and cheating are necessary to succeed and
2. teenagers are three times more likely than those older than forty to hold this belief.[1]

The result is that the line between what is considered right and wrong is becoming blurred. Lacking clear ethical standards to guide them, more and more leaders are making decisions based on what is expedient and what best serves their personal interests.

The preoccupation with greed has become so pervasive in our society that a major network television show titled "American Greed" is aired in prime-time. This program chronicles the numerous scams and schemes that have recently shattered the dreams of so many innocent people.

The advent of severe global competition and the acceleration of change are only making the situation worse. Many boards of directors are reacting to these trends by putting additional pressure on their management teams to improve short-term operating and financial results. With insufficient time to obtain the desired results and in fear of losing their jobs, the temptation is for managers to take shortcuts and do whatever it takes.

Even during the dark days of the Great Recession of 2008–2010, greed and insensitivity toward others flourished. In reaction to the precipitous decline in consumer spending, American business as a whole cut labor expenses far more than it lost in revenue.[2] By the end of the fourth quarter of 2008, corporate profitability soared to the highest levels in decades. At the same time, massive layoffs continued and countless other workers who kept their jobs had their hours reduced and/or took pay cuts. The result: millions of families lost their homes.[3]

It's interesting to note that in 2009, the worst year of the Great Recession, the CEOs of the fifty firms that laid off the most workers averaged 42 percent more pay than their peers at the Standard & Poor's five hundred firms.[4]

Another disturbing trend is the deterioration of empathy for others among young people. Sara Konrath, a researcher at the University of Michigan's Institute of Social Research, reviewed seventy-two previous studies that measured empathy among some fourteen thousand college students during the past thirty years. What she found is startling: college students today show 40 percent less empathy versus students in the 1980s and 1990s.[5]

In short, excessive greed and a lack of caring for others are fostering the proliferation of "dog-eat-dog" attitudes in our society. These attitudes are expressed by the following popular sayings:

- "The only reason we exist is to make a profit"
- "The end justifies the means"
- "Do whatever it takes"
- "Anything's legal as long as you don't get caught"
- "Nice guys finish last"
- "You have to watch out for your own interests first because other people are watching out for theirs."
- "Every man for himself"
- "It's good enough"

In the past few years we've seen what happens when "dog-eat-dog" attitudes prevail in organizations—fraudulent accounting practices, dangerous ingredients substituted in the manufacture of children's toys, the near collapse of our financial system, the failure to issue timely recalls for known safety defects in automobiles, and un-safe operations allowed in mining and off-shore drilling operations.

It's no wonder that the general public's perception of business leaders is at an all-time low. The bottom line is that leaders are increasingly being perceived as primarily interested in feathering their own nests at the expense of those they are expected to serve. The danger is that this selfish attitude becomes the norm.

Thankfully, "dog-eat-dog" attitudes do not exist in every organization. A majority of business leaders operate ethically and have a "caring for others" spirit.

There is hope that the movement toward a "dog-eat-dog" world can be reversed. It's encouraging to note from recent surveys that a majority of Americans want to return to the country's moral core—the values of honesty, integrity, decency, compassion for others, and hard work.[6] This is a great point upon which to start building a better future.

Chapter Two

What It's Like to Lead in a "Dog-Eat-Dog" World

Leading in a "dog-eat-dog," endangered world is extremely difficult and stressful. First and foremost, leaders, especially those in the lower and middle management ranks, live in constant fear of losing their jobs from reorganizing, downsizing, acquisitions, and periodic cost-cutting. Even if they're good performers, the threat of layoff is constantly hanging over their heads. The resulting stress is not only harmful to their well-being, but it also affects the welfare of their loved ones.

> In a "dog-eat-dog" world, people feel expendable.

Second, leaders are constantly under the gun to make their revenue and profit targets. Corporate America continues to have a fixation on quarterly results. The fact is that few people are allowed to keep their jobs when they experience three or four sub-par performance quarters in a row unless there are significant extenuating circumstances.

The responsibility for loved ones is what makes the threat of unemployment so onerous. Most lower and middle level leaders do not have sufficient savings to tide their families over for a lengthy period if they lose their job.

The handwriting is on the wall! The paternalistic days of the corporate world are gone forever. There is no job security! In addition, workers cannot count on company-funded pension plans to meet their retirement needs. In a few years, such plans will be non-existent. Somehow people will have to remain employed as long as possible and along the way save enough for retirement.

> In a "dog-eat-dog" world, everyone is trying to gain advantage over others.

With the feeling that there is no job security, the pressure to succeed is extraordinary. This in itself is very stressful. But, unfortunately, a leader often has the added burden of having to cope with one or more unscrupulous team members who may 1) withhold/distort information so they look good relative to the leader, 2) spread false or even malicious rumors about the leader's character, and 3) sabotage the leader's efforts. Some unethical people will stoop to almost anything to get ahead.

Yes, working in a "dog-eat-dog" world is very stressful. The normal human reaction is to find some way to relieve the pressure. Unfortunately, a number of leaders come to the conclusion that the only possibility is to succumb to "dog-eat-dog" tactics such as taking shortcuts, covering up, and cheating.

The good news is that there is an excellent alternative approach for becoming a successful leader without compromising your values. This is the subject of this book.

Chapter Three

There Is a Better Way— The Core Strategy

Opportunity awaits those who are willing to lead in a manner diametrically opposed to what occurs in our "dog-eat-dog" world. More than ever, people today long for competent leaders who strive to do the right things and have a caring attitude for their personnel. Leaders who are willing to approach their jobs in this fashion stand a far better chance of winning the loyalty and wholehearted cooperation of their people than those who lack integrity and are insensitive.

In this book you will learn about a powerful core strategy that will enable you to succeed by being an ethical, "caring for others" leader. **This strategy does not guarantee success, but it does dramatically improve the odds that you will reach your highest potential as a leader.**

The ECL Core Strategy for Success

Chapter Four

The Core Strategy: "E" for Ethics, "C" for Caring for Others, "L" for Lifelong Learning

If you were to Google the words, "how to be a successful leader," the result would be more than eighteen million references. With such an abundance of information, how do you determine what to concentrate on to reach your highest potential as a leader?

There are three basic approaches for focusing your leadership development efforts.

1. Competency Approach—doing research to identify the skills of outstanding leaders and then seeking to acquire similar expertise.

2. Modeling Approach—observing how successful leaders act and then patterning your own behavior accordingly.

3. Values Approach—identifying and internalizing the key personal and moral values that will guide you in your leadership efforts.

Core Strategy for Success

Core Strategy for Success advocates the adoption of three critically important leadership values as your primary guideposts for how to successfully lead others: "E" for Ethics, "C" for Caring for Others, and "L" for Lifelong Learning.

The ECL Core Strategy for Success provides a foundation upon which to build leadership success over the long haul. When a leader is both ethical and has a "caring for others" spirit, he or she fosters trust, integrity, respect, and loyalty throughout the organization. This, in turn, inspires people to give their best and work unselfishly as a team to achieve challenging objectives.

For the full potential of an organization to be realized, however, leaders must be knowledgeable in various functional disciplines such as strategic planning, operations, sales and marketing, and finance. This is where the "L" (for Lifelong Learning) in the Core Strategy for Success applies. Competence in any area comes from having a passion for continuous learning. A good leader will keep abreast of the best practices and the latest trends that affect his or her business. In addition, he or she will inspire others in the organization to do the same. The bottom line is that inspired, knowledgeable employees can achieve extraordinary accomplishments.

When the three leadership values of the Core Strategy are presented in a formula format, this is the result:

ECL Core Strategy for Success:

**E (Ethics) + C (Caring for Others) = inspired employees
+ L (Lifelong Learning) = long-term success**

You're invited to use this formula as *your* core strategy for success—success measured not only by what you achieve in your career, but also by how you live your life along the way.

Core Strategy #1: "E" for Ethics

Chapter Five

Leadership Ethics Defined

"Ideals are like stars; you will not succeed in touching them with your hands. But like the seafaring man on the desert of waters, you choose them as your guides, and following them you will reach your destiny."

—Carl Schurz

The first component of the ECL Core Strategy for Success is represented by the letter "E" for Ethics. This is **the most important leadership value of all!**

"Most definitions of ethics relate to rules, standards, and moral principles regarding what is right or wrong in specific situations."[7] More specifically, leadership ethics is the *expected standard(s) of behavior* of individuals responsible for the activities of others. The standards guide the leader's choices and actions.

> ECL Core Strategy:
>
> **"E" for Ethics**
> *"C" for Caring for Others*
> *"L" for Lifelong Learning*

High ethical standards in leadership evolve from the values of what is right, good, honest, and fair in our society. The standards apply to one's personal conduct and how others should be treated (e.g. employees, customers, vendors, and shareholders). Some examples of expected ethical behavior by leaders include:

1. putting the welfare of the organization and employees ahead of self-interest,
2. playing by the rules,
3. telling the truth,
4. keeping promises, and
5. being fair.

The purpose of this section is to help you succeed in your career by being ethical in all your dealings.

Chapter Six

The Importance of Ethics to Leadership Success

"Your deeds are your destiny."

—Deepak Chopra

The most important imperative for long-term leadership success is be ethical—doing what is right, good, honest, and fair.

> Leadership success is all about relationships, and good relationships can be developed only if there is mutual trust.

Why is being ethical so important for achieving leadership success? It all has to do with *building trust* with your colleagues. The one common denominator of business is trust. It is as simple as this—if you maintain high standards of ethical behavior, you will be trusted by the people you interact with. Trust is the bond that holds relationships together in an organization. Without it, nothing functions well.

J. William Pfeiffer, writing in *Handbook of Structured Experiences for Human Relations Training*, says, "Only trust will create people who are able to say, 'Yes, let's try that;' to believe that corporate information has been presented accurately; to feel it's safe to share ideas without being ridiculed; and to feel supported for their efforts, even if their plans fail . . . at this point, positive leadership can engage people to become more efficient and productive."

Trust is the key to developing the strong working relationships that are necessary for people to work unselfishly together to achieve common objectives. Dr. William Schultz, a noted psychologist who developed "truth-in-management strategies" at Proctor and Gamble and NASA, says, "Nothing increases work group compatibility like mutual trust and honesty."[8] He adds, "When trust and honesty are fundamental values in an organization, individuals are more willing to work as a team."[9]

No one will continually give 100 percent to someone they don't trust. In the short-term they may be forced to produce out of fear of losing their jobs. But, over the long haul, people will not consistently perform above the call of duty when leadership trust is lacking.

When people trust their leader, energy is diverted from worrying and complaining to more productive endeavors such as finding better ways of accomplishing tasks. In time, a powerful success force enables the team to do extraordinary things. This, in turn, attracts outstanding people from other departments who want to work in such an environment.

> *Trust is absolutely key to long-term success.*
>
> **Jim Burke**
> (Former Chairman and CEO of Johnson & Johnson)

Having strong ethics has always been an important driver of success in business. Today, with the globalization of business and the dispersion of work functions and customer bases, managers must collaborate in real-time with colleagues from different countries and cultures, often thousands of miles apart. And these managers seldom, if ever, have face-to-face contact with the people on whom they depend for results.

"Remote leadership" is extremely challenging because leaders are forced to rely primarily on impersonal forms of communication, such as the telephone, e-mail, and tele-conferencing. If a leader's foreign colleagues ever detect even the slightest hint of favoritism, incomplete disclosure, or dishonesty on his or her

> *The only way to build trust professionally or personally is being trustworthy.*
>
> **Gerard Arpey**
> (CEO, American Airlines)

part, it will create a breach of trust that is very difficult to repair because of the inability to immediately work problems out face-to-face.

According to Craig E. Weatherup, the former CEO of Pepsi Bottling Group, Inc., "People will tolerate honest mistakes, but if you violate their trust you will find it very difficult to ever regain their confidence . . . that is the reason you need to treat trust as your most precious asset."

It's the leader's role to build organizational trust by being ethical. **It cannot be stressed strongly enough how important it is for the leader to set the example for ethical behavior.** Only then will others act in a similar manner.

The fact is that a leader's ethics really do matter in the world of work. The same is true for the overall business enterprise. Companies that have a reputation for being ethical in their dealings with customers, employees, suppliers, and share-holders have a major competitive advantage. To illustrate, one of America's greatest start-up corporations, FedEx, earned the trust of the public by doing the right things for its customers, even when it was costly to do so.

Occasionally, FedEx misdirects a few packages. Sometimes, this causes a serious problem for a customer. Such was the case for a large pharmaceutical company that was holding a national sales rally in Los Angeles. Salespeople, like everyone else, thrive on recognition, especially receiving awards in front of their colleagues. Unfortunately, several boxes of awards were sent to Chicago instead of Los Angeles. This meant that unless drastic action was taken immediately, the awards would not arrive in Los Angeles in time for the winners to receive them at a formal gala dinner.

> *Each time you insist that your personnel operate in an ethical manner, it moves your organization toward greater success.*

Without hesitation, the Chicago FedEx employees quickly loaded the boxes of awards on an empty jet and arranged to have it flown to Los Angeles in hope that it would arrive on time for the ceremony. The boxes were rushed from the airport to the hotel ballroom by several FedEx managers. The dinner had already begun. As the managers sheepishly approached the podium with the awards, they fully expected to receive a round of boos from the audience. But instead, the crowd of nearly one thousand people broke out in loud applause.

The details of this unusual effort to correct a serious service problem were quickly spread by word-of-mouth throughout the entire FedEx system. Soon employees everywhere understood that they were expected to do the right thing for customers, even when it is inconvenient or costly to do so.

Another classic illustration that ethics is good for the overall business enterprise is the serious incident that occurred in the fall of 1982. It was discovered that seven people on Chicago's West Side had died from taking Johnson and Johnson's Tylenol capsules that had been laced with cyanide. Even though it was obvious from the start that the tampering with the product occurred after it left the control of the company, Johnson & Johnson took responsibility for the problem by immediately halting Tylenol sales and recalling more than 31 million bottles of the medication at an estimated cost of $200 million.

The reaction from the world-wide press was quite unexpected. Instead of criticizing Johnson & Johnson for somehow allowing the problem to occur, a vast majority of the world's newspapers applauded the company for being honest with the public and acting decisively without regard to the cost involved. Johnson & Johnson quickly marshaled its resources and developed tamper-proof packaging that soon became the standard for the entire industry. Within six weeks, Tylenol was back on the store shelves, and it wasn't long until the company regained its market share. Best of all, and most importantly for their business, Johnson & Johnson gained the reputation of being an ethical company.

Several years after the Tylenol incident, the Vanguard Group, Inc. (seller of mutual fund shares) announced that it had implemented policies to prevent late trading abuses on the stock exchanges. The interesting fact is not so much that Vanguard acted to eliminate the abuses, but that it did so several years before the change was required by law and well before it was done by a competitor. This and other ethical decisions by Vanguard throughout the years helped it build and maintain an image of trust with the public—trust that has enabled it to become the largest seller of stock index funds in the world.

In the cases of FedEx, Johnson & Johnson, and Vanguard, it was costly to make the right choices for their customers, but in the long run their ethical policies paid off handsomely.

The concept that it pays for companies to be ethical was substantiated by several studies conducted by Remi Trudel and June Cotte. They found that "consumers, in general, are willing to pay a slight premium for ethically made goods and consumers with high ethical expectations are willing to pay a substantial premium."[10]

Besides standing behind their products with customers, even if it is costly to do so, companies need to demonstrate a high level of ethics with their other constituents—employees, vendors, and the public in general. Some of the approaches for doing so include the following:

1. Operating in a safe manner.
2. Ensuring diversity in hiring, training, and promotions.
3. Following "green" environmental practices.
4. Paying vendors and producers fairly and in a timely manner.

Whole Foods Market Inc. is an excellent example of a company that goes out of its way to act according to the above principles. It even applies its philosophy of social responsibility to producer communities in developing countries, where it sources some of its products. There are several unique features of its Whole Trade Program:[11]

1. Helping to fight poverty by donating 1 percent of sales to its Whole Foods Foundation to provide loans and tangible support for community projects.
2. "Compassionate sourcing" in which the company buys from small operations that have limited outlets for their products.

Starbucks, the world's leading coffee retailer, is also dedicated to the policy of being ethical by adhering to a policy of "compassionate sourcing." Recently, the company issued a statement that read, "84 percent of our coffee last year was sourced from farmers who are good to their workers, community, and planet . . . our goal is to ensure that 100 percent is ethically sourced by 2015."

My favorite story of a major corporation being ethical by demonstrating its social responsibility happened a few years ago when Merck & Co., Inc. decided to spend millions of dollars to cure the second leading infectious cause of blindness—onchocerciasis. This disease, often called "River Blindness," is transmitted to humans from the bite of the black fly. Over time, parasitic worms form and spread causing a strong immune system response that destroys human tissue, such as the eyes.

Merck got involved in this public health issue in 1975 when it inadvertently discovered that a fungus taken from a turf sample from a golf course in Japan produced a chemical toxic to parasitic worms. This discovery led to the development of an anti-parasitic medication named Ivermectin.

Merck was soon faced with a serious ethical dilemma. Producing and distributing Ivermectin was not economically viable, but it was the right thing to do to cure River Blindness. The market for the drug was very limited. Most of the people afflicted by the disease lived in the under-developed nations of Africa. They did not have the means to pay for the drug, neither did the African governments have the resources to help.

Initially, Merck sought assistance of third-party payers such as the World Health Organization and the U.S. Department of State. Even several United States Senators were asked to support Congressional action to sponsor the distribution of the drug. All these efforts failed. Finally, Dr. Roy Vagelos, Chairman of Merck, decreed that his company would donate

Ivermectin to all who needed it and would do so for as long as required.

By 2002 it was estimated that more than sixteen million people in Africa had been spared infection from River Blindness because of the use of the free drug. And best of all, Merck set the example for other pharmaceutical companies. Soon they, too, began donating drugs to prevent malaria and other diseases prevalent in developing nations.

Some companies even make it a practice to donate a portion of the revenue from each product sale to support ethical causes. Toms Shoes is a great example of such generosity. As noted on their Web site, they give a pair of shoes to a child in need for every one purchased—one for one.

> *Greed destroys wealth. Trust and integrity, by contrast, foster prosperity.*
>
> **Patricia Aburdene**
> (Author of *Megatrends 2010*)

It's noteworthy that all the companies cited above—FedEx, Johnson & Johnson, Vanguard, Whole Foods, Toms, Merck, and Starbucks—are leaders in their respective fields. According to recent research, it's not a coincidence that such companies are very successful. In one landmark study of the five hundred largest U.S. public corporations, it was found that those firms having strong ethics policies were more profitable than those that did not.[12] *The Journal of Business and Economic Research* adds, "There is a positive correlation between an organization's ethical behaviors and its bottom line results."

Dov Seidman, a leading ethics-in-business consultant, describes why good corporate behavior is playing such an important role in determining a company's success: "Globalization has made it increasingly difficult for companies to differentiate themselves based on their products alone . . . whatever your product or service might be, chances are that someone on the other side of the world can copy and sell it for less money . . . all the more important, then, that companies compete by striving to be good corporate citizens and by operating ethically." [13]

Yes, ethical behavior is good for your career and yes, ethics is good for the success of the overall business enterprise.

Besides the business reasons for having good ethics, there is another important reason for always striving to do the right thing. Ethics is good for your *personal well-being*.

Television commentator Ted Koppel says, "There's harmony and inner peace to be found in following a moral compass that points in the same direction regardless of fashion or trend." John Wooden, the legendary UCLA basketball coach added, "There is no pillow as soft as a clear conscience."

There's absolutely no real satisfaction in succeeding by cheating and harming others, but there is a great deal of satisfaction from achieving success by doing things the right way. More importantly, following the rules and making the right choices enables you to maintain your personal integrity.

In short, *ethics is good for the soul!* And when your soul is healthy, so is your overall well-being.

There's another reason for you to live an ethical life. In today's world, any serious breach of ethics on your part could very well be exposed for everyone to see, now and for generations to come.

> *A good name is seldom regained. When character is gone, one of the richest jewels of life is lost forever.*
>
> **J. Hanes**

In the old days, if you did something really bad you merely packed up and moved to a far away location and started a new life. Chances were good that no one would ever discover your "little secret." But today, with everyone "Googling" everyone else and checking your electronic footprint on the Web, *your record will follow you to the grave and well beyond!*

If you're involved with social media such as Twitter, Facebook, and LinkedIn, keep in mind that you can't control what happens to the information once you send it. When you press "send" there is no way to retract or modify the message content. Worse yet, you have no idea what will be done with the information.

We're living in an age when even a not-so-serious breach of ethics can ruin one's career and personal life. For example, an offhand comment to an acquaintance about a confidential matter at work could be posted on an industry blog and cause serious consequences for you and your company. It's also possible that a cell phone photo or video of your behavior at a private party could become a permanent part of your Internet search results.

Social media such as YouTube, Facebook, and Twitter have dramatically accelerated the rate by which a comment or message by a public figure or even an ordinary person can be picked up and broadcasted to millions by the national media. It's surprising how many such communications are misleading, incorrect, and even inflammatory in nature. Even worse is the growing number of attempts to deliberately ruin someone's life by electronically spreading malicious rumors about his or her character.

Therefore, before communicating in any manner, make sure you have all the facts. Double-check to make sure they're correct. Then express your thoughts in a manner that adheres to strict ethical standards. Finally, always assume that what you say or write will be broadcast to your bosses, your associates, your competitors, and even to everyone around the world.

As the English author Ernest Bramah said, "A reputation for a thousand years may depend upon the conduct of a single moment." What a powerful thought to remember!

In review, there are four important reasons for leading an ethical life:

1. Ethics is good for your career.
2. Ethics is good for the business enterprise.
3. Ethics is good for your soul.
4. Ethics is good for preserving your reputation.

The fifth reason for you to lead an ethical life is that *it is the right thing to do.* This is the most important reason of all! An ethical person does the right thing even though it may not be in his or her best interest to do so. As the famous Indian leader Mohandas Gandhi said, "It is the action, not the fruit of the action, that's important . . . you have to do the right thing . . . it may not be in your power or it may not be in your time that there'll be any fruit . . . but that doesn't mean you stop doing the right thing . . . you may never know what results come from your action . . . but if you do nothing, there will be no result."[13]

Taken together, the five important reasons for being ethical provide a compelling argument for always doing what is right, good, honest, and fair.

Despite all the important reasons for being ethical, some people seem to live on the edge by doing the right thing when it's convenient to do so or when it doesn't cost them anything.

Such people tend to be extremely short-sighted and self-centered.

> It's the height of absurdity to sow little but weeds in the first half of one's lifetime and expect to harvest a valuable crop in the second half.
>
> **Henry Wadsworth Longfellow**
> (19th century poet)

According to Ken Blanchard and Phil Hodges, writing in the book *Lead like Jesus: Lessons from the Greatest Role Model of All Time,* "A heart motivated by self-interest looks at the world as a 'give a little, take a lot' proposition." They continue by saying, "People with hearts motivated by self-interest put their own agenda—safety, status, and gratification—ahead of those affected by their thoughts and actions." Such an attitude invariably leads to unethical behavior.

Some selfish people justify their unethical behavior by saying that nice guys finish last. Dr. Norman Vincent Peale, the renowned twentieth century Methodist minister and author of *The Power of Positive Thinking*, had a strong counter to this philosophy. He said, "Nice guys may appear to finish last, but usually they're running in a different race to achieve success."[14] Dr. Peale backed up his statement with a story of an art director of a magazine who was fired because he refused to work on a project that included pornographic material. After nearly a year searching for new work, he found an even better job. Ironically, it was the strong recommendation of the art director's former boss that played a key role in making the new job possible. Apparently he respected the man's character. As Dr. Peale said, "The art director's patience paid off, because he was running in a different race."[15]

My interpretation of what Dr. Peale meant by "running a different race" is that career success is not all about making more and more money. Rather, it has more to do with how a person lives his or her life in terms of doing what is right, good, honest, and fair.

> *Forget about who finishes first and who finishes last. Decent, honorable people finish races—and their lives—in grand style and with respect.*
>
> **Jon M. Huntsman**
> (21st century American businessman and philanthropist)

Jon M. Huntsman, chairman and founder of Huntsman Corporation, talks about the race for success in a slightly different way. In his book, *Winners Never Cheat,* Huntsman notes, "There are basically three kinds of people: the unsuccessful, the temporarily successful, and those who become successful and remain successful. The difference, I'm convinced, is character." The message here is that it's possible for a person to lie and cheat his or her way to the top. But, it takes character to remain there.

People who live unethical lives do not realize that usually their actions come to haunt them. And the haunting will be very painful emotionally in terms of estranged loved ones, hatred from former work associates, a soiled reputation, and worst of all, a feeling of despair and loneliness.

In addition, those who have fraudulently clawed their way to the top are often ruined financially in the end. That's why the age-old sayings of "You reap what you sow," and "What goes around comes around," are so applicable in everyone's life. These catchy statements imply that if you consistently cheat and abuse people, someday you're likely to be repaid in kind when you least expect it. The converse is also true; if you live an ethical life and consistently treat everyone with respect and dignity, quite often your good deeds facilitate positive things happening to you. The one positive thing that will occur for sure is that you will feel good about yourself. This is priceless!

Core Strategy for Success

Therefore, my charge to you is this:

Live your life by the highest ethical standards. Throughout your career you will be tempted and/or pressured to do the expedient, to shade the truth, to distort performance results, to overlook compliance with rules and regulations, or to violate other ethical standards. Stand firm, don't waiver, and someday you can look back at your accomplishments with pride and satisfaction; for you will have succeeded by "doing things the right way" without violating the fundamental values of what is right, good, honest, and fair in our society. More than anything else, your legacy will be that you inspired others to live their lives in a similar fashion.

Chapter Seven

How to Live an Ethical Life

"In matters of principle, stand like a rock."

—Thomas Jefferson

There are five basic actions that a person should take to live an ethical life:

1. Make a personal commitment to always do what is right, good, honest, and fair. This requires that you say to yourself, "I'm going to keep my commitment, no matter what!"

In an interview in *Leadership Guide Magazine,* motivational speaker and consultant Jon Gordon was asked how one can remain ethical in today's ever-changing and turbulent times. His response: "You do it by periodically asking yourself what you want as your legacy . . . knowing how you want to be remembered helps you decide how to live today."

2. Learn how to be ethical. Once you're committed to living ethically, you must learn how to act in a manner that is right, good, honest, and fair.

Learning how to be ethical is not something easily acquired from reading or even taking a course on the subject. Aristotle said, "The spirit of morality is awakened in the individual only through the witness and conduct of a moral person."[16] The practical application of Aristotle's thought in your life is that you should observe how ethical people act and then pattern your own behavior after what you see them do.

I learned the importance of being ethical from occasionally listening to my dad talk business on the telephone at home with his plant managers. For some reason, which at the time I did not comprehend, he often allowed me to lie quietly on the floor of our den while he conversed. After the calls, he made it a practice to tell me about the issues he was facing, especially those involving leadership and ethics. Now, when I reflect on those experiences, I realize that Dad was demonstrating his love for me by providing invaluable learning opportunities. He was a wonderful ethical role model.

> *To set a lofty example is the richest bequest a man can leave behind.*
>
> **S. Smiles**
> (19th century Scottish author and reformer)

In addition to my father, I had another great role model to emulate early in my business career and that was Frank Borman, the President of Eastern Airlines. I had the fortunate opportunity to serve as his administrative manager when the company was at its pinnacle of success—serving more passengers in North America than any other airline. Prior to working for Eastern, Borman was a hero of the early American Space Program when he commanded Apollo 8, the first spacecraft to fly around the moon.

By the way he lived his life, Borman taught me a great deal about honesty and integrity.

Just as I decided years ago to emulate my father's and Borman's behavior in life, you, too, can seek out ethical role models. They might be one of your coaches, a relative, or someone you work for. Listen to what they say but, most importantly, observe how they act and how their actions favorably affect others. Then, make a conscious decision to be like them.

3. Utilize the Golden Rule as your primary ethics guideline. Once you've committed to living an ethical life and learned how to do so, it's helpful to have an overall ethics guideline to assist you in determining if a contemplated action is ethical.

Probably the most succinct and universal ethics guideline is the *Golden Rule:* "Do unto others as you would have them do unto you." I was surprised to learn that the *Golden Rule*

> *We have committed the Golden Rule to memory; let us now commit it to life.*
>
> **Edwin Markham**
> (20th century poet)

is endorsed, in one way or another, by all the great religious faiths of the world—Buddhism, Christianity, Hinduism, Islam, and Judaism.[17] For centuries, the idea of treating others as you want to be treated has been influential among peoples of uniquely diverse cultures. This fact strongly suggests that the *Golden Rule* is an important universal moral truth.

Therefore, whenever you're faced with a decision that affects others, ask yourself: "How would I like to be treated in this exact situation?" If you're unwilling to be treated in the same way you're considering to treat others, then you would be violating the rule.

This raises the issue of just how do people want to be treated? Human beings in all cultures want to be: 1) respected, 2) trusted, 3) valued, 4) noticed, 5) heard, and 6) treated fairly. It's helpful to keep this in mind when considering how the *Golden Rule* applies to a decision or action that impacts people in other countries.

Supplement the *Golden Rule* with other ethics guidelines. Limiting yourself to the *Golden Rule* as your only ethics guideline has an important drawback. It may not cover all situations where there is an issue involving ethics. For example, what if you're okay personally with a contemplated action in terms of how you'd like to be treated, but the action violates the spirit of the law or is perceived to be unfair by others? Or, what if your action is based on assumptions that are not quite truthful? Such valid issues need to be carefully explored beyond merely applying the *Golden Rule*.

> Your ethical and moral values must be absolute—you must believe in them so much that they override your ego, your weaknesses, and your rationalizations.

There are several additional ethics guidelines that can be used to supplement the *Golden Rule* to provide a more comprehensive basis for determining whether a contemplated action is the right thing to do. In an effort to assist you in this decision-making process I have reformatted the guidelines into questions. I call them the Ethics Guideline Questions. Ask them of yourself before you act.

1. *Does my contemplated action violate any laws?* This applies not only to the letter of the law, but also to the spirit and intent of it. A "yes" answer to the question precludes the necessity to continue with the other guideline questions. No one should deliberately break the law. But in life, things often are not so cut and dried. It's possible for an action to be legal while at the same time being unethical.

   Unfortunately, some people use the legality question as their only guideline to determine whether a contemplated action is ethical. In their minds, if the action can stand the test of the law, nothing else matters. The maintenance of high standards of ethics, however, requires the review of other important considerations such as an assessment of potential harm or inequity from an action. The legal question should therefore serve only as a starting point in your deliberations to determine what the right thing to do is. If your answer to question number one is "no" always proceed to ask yourself the following additional questions.

2. *Does my contemplated action potentially harm anyone,* including me? The harm can be physical, economic, or even psychological. It was the ancient Greek physician Hippocrates who said, "Above all, do no harm."

3. *Is it fair to those who will be affected by my action?* This question is derived from the Rotary International motto that has been used for years by millions of people worldwide in their decision-making. Fairness means being just in the dealings with people.

4. *How would I like to be treated in a similar situation?* This is a rephrasing of the *Golden Rule:* "Do unto others as you would have them do unto you."

5. *Does my behavior reflect favorably on how I would like to be remembered?* If not, don't do it! A somewhat related question would be, "How would I feel if my action was reported in my local newspaper or on the Internet?"

6. *Will I feel a sense of self-respect and dignity from what I did?* Writing in *The Heart of a Leader*, Ken Blanchard says, "You can't go against your image of

yourself and what you think is right without feeling bad."

> *The time is always right to do what is right.*
>
> **Martin Luther King**

Since most decisions involving ethical matters do not have to be made on the spot, there is usually sufficient time to contemplate your alternatives based on thinking through the answers to the Ethics Guideline Questions. Resist the urge to make a quick decision that involves ethical issues. Usually it takes some time to reflect on all the ramifications of such a decision. You may also want to discuss your quandary with someone you respect and trust. More than anything, you want to do the right thing, so take whatever time is necessary to think things through. As Charles Swindoll says in his book, *David: a Man of Passion and Destiny,* "Do nothing until it is right, and then do it with all your might."

However, if you are in a situation where a quick decision has to be made and you don't feel good about it, simply say "no" and do whatever is necessary to remove yourself from the situation. A polite way to buy time to reflect on your decision is to say, "I

> *The power of choosing good and evil is within the reach of all.*
>
> **Origen Adamantius**
> (3rd century scholar and theologian)

need a little time to think about it, and I'll get back with you later." Or, if necessary, you may have to be more direct by saying, "This is wrong, and I won't do it." By stopping and backing off, you give your moral compass a chance to right itself. The *Tao Te Ching* text (ancient, classic Chinese manuscript central to Taoism and Chinese Buddhism) says, "He who knows when to stop is preserved from peril." This often takes courage, but it may prevent you from doing something that you will long regret.

It has been my experience that the biggest trap that people face in the ethics area is what I call the "just-this-one-time" rationalization. Do not fall into this trap. Some of the most unethical things people do are justified with the self-promise that "I will do it only this one time and never again." Once you have acted in an unethical manner, it's a lot easier to do it again and again. Also, one time is all it takes to ruin your reputation and career.

Another ethics trap that some people fall for is the "everybody else does it" excuse. This dangerous rationalization is especially seductive in highly competitive international industries where certain financially weak players traditionally use kickbacks and bribes to obtain much needed business. The temptation is to match the unethical behavior instead of taking the high road of competing strictly on product innovation, quality, and legal volume discounting programs.

In 2007 Siemens Corporation hired Peter Löscher to clean up a sales and marketing culture that relied on kickbacks and bribes to obtain business outside North America. He quickly set a new tone by insisting that everyone comply with the company's ethical code of conduct. In sales and marketing meetings he made it crystal clear it was no longer acceptable to justify immoral behavior based on the rationale that it's the only way to do business in countries that operate by a different set of rules. "My experience leads to a contrary conclusion," says Löscher. "Ethics apply universally . . . so stick to your principles and try to win, not by cheating, but by out-innovating your competitors."[18]

The results of his efforts have been amazing. Siemens went from a very low ethics compliance ranking to an exceptionally high one.[19]

Unethical behavior often starts by a person doing a small thing that does not seem very important at the time, but later escalates into much bigger things. The trick is not to start in the first place. Andy Grove, the long-time CEO of Intel, says, "Being ethical isn't an easy principle to stick to . . . there are always many reasons—better to call them excuses—to compromise a little here or a little there . . . we may reason that people are not ready to hear the truth or the bad news, that the time is not right, or whatever . . . giving in to those tempting rationalizations usually leads to conduct that can be ethically wrong." [20]

There will be occasions when the answers to one or more of the following Ethics Guideline Questions are in conflict with the others.

- Is it legal?
- Does it harm anyone?
- Is it fair?
- How would I like to be treated in a similar situation?
- Does my behavior reflect how I would like to be remembered?
- Will I respect myself for what I did?

When the answers to the questions are in conflict, determine which criterion is most important and seems to override all the others. Then make your decision based on that judgment.

So far I've presented three actions that a person must take to live an ethical life: 1) make a personal commitment to be ethical in all your dealings, 2) learn how to be ethical, and 3) utilize the Ethics Guideline Questions to assist you in decision-making. The fourth action you must take is to develop the habit of being ethical.

4. Develop the habit of being ethical. The habit of always acting ethically is acquired in the same fashion as any other good habit. After committing yourself to being ethical, you have to practice doing the right thing by repeating the appropriate behavior over and over again until it becomes natural.

> *We are what we repeatedly do.*
>
> **Aristotle**

C. S. Lewis, a noted twentieth century British novelist, said, "Every time you make a choice you are turning the central part of you, the part that chooses, into something a little different from what it was before . . . and taking your life as a whole, with all your innumerable choices, all your life long you are slowly turning this central thing either into a heavenly creature or into a hellish creature."

People who have tried to lose weight or quit smoking know it's not easy to break a deep-seated bad habit. The same principle applies to a person who has previously practiced "situational ethics"—doing the right thing when others are looking or when it doesn't cost them anything. It was John Luther who said, "Most talents are to some extent a gift . . . good character, by contrast, is not given to us . . . we have to build it piece by piece—by thought, choice, courage, and determination." The nineteenth century English historian and novelist James A. Froude added, "You can't dream yourself into character; you must hammer and forge yourself one."

> *The law of harvest is to reap more than you sow. Sow an act, and you reap a habit; sow a habit, and you reap a character; sow a character and you reap a destiny.*

5. Surround yourself with people of integrity. Finally, in your effort to be an ethical person, it's helpful to have work associates and friends who share your ethical values. It was George Washington who said, "Associate with men of good quality, if you esteem your own reputation." Associating with honorable people has the added benefit of providing a ready source of encouragement and support when you're faced with making difficult decisions with ethical implications.

At work, try to forge close relationships with key people known for their character. After establishing mutual trust with them, support each other in working toward ensuring that all operations are conducted in an ethical manner.

Chapter Eight

A Classic Ethics Dilemma

"Have the courage to say no. Have the courage to face the truth. Do the right thing. These are the magic keys to living your life with integrity."

—W. Clement Stone

Doing what is right, good, honest, and fair during your career takes considerable determination and courage. You will be repeatedly tempted and/or urged to do things that are unethical. Torn between upholding your ethical standards and loyalty to your superior and even losing your job, you must make a choice. You can compromise yourself by doing what's expedient, or you can stand up for what you believe and take the consequences.

As you read the following story, keep in mind that what happened to Alice could happen to you. As background, she was a finance manager in a large international corporation. Although this incident is based on facts presented in the media, the names, dialogue, and setting are fictitious.

The Dilemma

It was a dark, cold winter morning on the Friday after the close of the business quarter, and Alice was driving to work. The radio weather forecast called for a bitter cold but sunny day. The thought of the coming sunshine seemed to pick up Alice's spirits a bit even though she was exhausted from tossing and turning the entire night.

Alice hadn't slept well because she kept thinking about the problem at work. It was a huge problem; the preliminary financial results for the quarter looked disastrous with sizable losses for the corporation's consolidated world-wide operations. When the press release announcing the unexpected loss was issued in a few days, the shocking news would cause a significant sell-off of the company's stock; and, worse yet, it would negatively impact the firm's credit ratings. This, in turn, would make it difficult, if not impossible, to raise much-needed capital for desired acquisitions.

When Alice arrived at work, she was surprised to find her boss, the Corporate Controller (John), anxiously waiting for her outside her office. His greeting of "Good morning, Alice" lacked its usual cheerful tone. In fact, John looked like he had slept in his clothes, and it was obvious he hadn't shaved. "We need to talk *now!*" he blurted.

"Ok," she said, "let's use my office. What's up?"

"It's about the results for the quarter, so you'd better shut the door."

Alice closed the door, turned, and found John staring pensively out the window. For a few moments he didn't say a word. Finally, he spoke in a low, gravelly voice, "I hardly slept at all last night."

"Me either."

John continued: "I was just about to go to bed when Bill (the CFO) called. He's asking us to fix the problem."

"Fix the problem?" Alice echoed with a quizzical look on her face.

"Yes, reclassify certain routine operating expenses as capital expenditures."

Alice looked pale as a ghost. "Why," she stammered, "that's against the accounting regulations."

> *The end never justifies the means!*

"I know, I know, but there's nothing else we can do. Bill says that we're all toast if we report the big loss. He promised me that this would be a one-time thing, and he wouldn't ask us to do it again."

"I hope you told him No, we won't do it."

John looked sheepish. "Not exactly. I told him that I didn't like it, but we'd do it just this one time. He even said that he'd remember our helpful attitude when it's bonus time."

"But I can't—"

"Don't make this difficult for me, Alice. Just take care of it, and there won't be any problems."

"Like what kind of problems?"

"Just do it!" John demanded as he abruptly left Alice's office.

As indicated earlier, you can obtain clarity on whether or not a contemplated action or decision is ethical by asking yourself the Ethics Guideline Questions. Take a moment to respond to the questions on the next page relative to the ethics issue of re-classifying certain normal operating expenses as capital expenditures.

> 1. Does the request violate any law?
>
> 2. Does it harm anyone?
>
> 3. Is it unfair?
>
> 4. Would I like to be treated the same way?
>
> 5. Is it how I would like to be remembered?
>
> 6. Would I respect myself for what I did?

On the basis of what is right or wrong ethically, the appropriate responses are "yes" for questions 1–3 and "no" for 4–6. Bottom line: altering the financial books is absolutely unethical, no matter how you look at it.

With this understanding, what should Alice do?

As difficult as it is, she must stand up for what is right, even if it puts her job in jeopardy. Obviously, this is a lot easier said than done when there is considerable financial risk involved for the whistleblower. Unfortunately, the real-life person in the episode did agree to cook the books and became party to one of the most serious cases of corporate fraud in American history. Not only was her career ruined, but she also received a prison sentence.

> *Integrity involves a price, but the cost pales in comparison with the cost of compromise.*
>
> **Paul Kroger**
> (Author)

It's easy to be ethical when it doesn't cost you anything. It's much more difficult to stand firm in your ethical beliefs when you know there may be negative consequences such as receiving a bad performance review, being by-passed for a desired promotion, or even being fired.

Losing out on something you really want is the price you may have to pay for being an ethical person.

The important take-away from this episode is this: if your manager asks you to do something you believe is unethical, you should first make sure of the facts, and then refuse to act unethically.

It cannot be stressed strongly enough how important it is to have all the facts before you make an issue out of what you believe is a significant ethics violation in your organization. As my dad was fond of saying, "Things are often not what they first appear to be." How true this is! Therefore, before claiming a violation, double-check to make sure that you have all the pertinent facts and that they are correct. Review corporate policies for guidance. In addition, seek the opinion of several close friends you work with. Armed with this background, politely confront your manager and present your case. If this fails, there are several appropriate strategies for being a whistleblower both within and outside your company.

In many corporations there are established procedures for anonymously reporting ethics violations. If you are fortunate enough to be employed by such an organization, let the system work for you. You may also want to reveal the situation to your mentor or a senior officer whom you trust.

If such efforts are to no avail, contact an outside attorney for guidance. He or she can inform you of the procedures for reporting fraud and bribery at publically traded companies. The SEC's Whistleblower Program under the Dodd-Frank Law permits individuals to go to federal court if they are retaliated against for revealing violations. The program also rewards the whistleblower with a percentage of the fines that are levied against the offending corporation. The Whistleblower Program has considerably strengthened the hand of employees who are willing to take a stand against unethical behavior in their companies.

If you work for a company that does not have a formal mechanism for reporting ethics violations, your best approach is to seek the counsel of a senior executive who is known for being ethical. He or she may elect to champion your cause. If this fails, seek outside legal advice.

Above all, do not remain in an unethical organization that you cannot change. Cut your losses by moving on to an employer that strives to be ethical. Obviously, the preferred exit strategy is to seek employment elsewhere while still employed. Only as a last resort should you abruptly resign without first obtaining a new job. The point is, there are many companies that strive to do the right thing. Such firms constantly seek competent, ethical people. Cast your destiny with one of them.

> *Try to work for an organization of people you admire.*
>
> **Warren Buffett**

There are several good places to look for companies that demonstrate high ethical values. The first one is the annual publication of the "100 Best Corporate Citizens" in *CRO Magazine*. The second source is the "World's Most Ethical Companies" list published each year by Ethisphere.

Research on the Internet is also an excellent way to learn about the ethical values of prospective employers. Job-oriented Web sites often feature comments by past and present employees of companies. Also, review corporate Web sites and Facebook and Twitter updates for possible clues about what companies are doing in the ethics area. If possible, secure the input of friends or acquaintances who work for firms you're interested in. Ask people to give you the straight story about how the top leaders are perceived by lower-level workers.

In summary, the overall lesson from the "Alice Episode" is: **Have the courage to stand firm in what you believe, no matter what! Go for long-term success. You'll never regret it!**

Chapter Nine

The Leader's Role in Ensuring High Ethical Standards

The greatest contribution leaders can make to society is to model ethical behavior.

The most important duty of a leader is to establish and maintain an ethical culture in his or her organization. This is a difficult task, especially during difficult economic times. But it can be done and here's how:

1. First and foremost, you (the leader), must set the example for others to follow by performing your duties in an ethical manner. You must insure that all your actions are above reproach by resisting the siren call of placing your own personal gain above that of your customers, employees, and shareholders.

You never know when your actions are observed and what influence they have on others. Leading others is like being on stage where your every action is carefully scrutinized. It's imperative, therefore, that you live by

> *Example is not the main thing in influencing others; it is the only thing.*
>
> **Albert Schweitzer**
> (20th century theologian and philosopher)

your values daily; only then can you insist that everyone else do the same.

As previously mentioned, most employees want to do what is right, good, honest, and fair when they make decisions. Your role as the leader is to empower them to take action based on these values and to back their decisions. The moment the maintenance of high ethical standards ceases to be the leader's top priority; the seeds of organizational failure are sown. Remember**, it all starts at the top!**

2. Make operating in an ethical manner the top priority of everyone in the organization. This means that doing the right thing ethically trumps maximizing short-term profitability.

    Once again, the overall tone for the "ethics first" core value is set by the attitude and example of the top leader. In addition, the corporate mission statement and the annual objectives should reflect this value.

    It is also advisable to develop an "Ethics Code of Conduct" for your organization. This is simply a list of principles and rules for how people are expected to act in the performance of their duties. One of the statements should be that employees are free to report ethical violations without fear of retribution.

3. Hire people who are ethical. Doing so is critically important for building an ethical operation. Since it's very difficult to get an existing employee who is used to shading the truth or using the system for personal advantage to change for the better, you're far better off hiring someone in the first place who is known for having character.

   Warren Buffett, one of the most successful investors of all time, has an interesting way of stressing this point to his staff. He says, "Use three primary criteria in hiring: integrity, intelligence, and energy . . . hire someone without the first and the other two will kill you." The message here is to insist that your hiring process is comprehensive and thorough. This includes having several key members of your staff interview each new-hire candidate and carefully perform reference checks.

4. Make the topic of "operating ethically" a central theme in all training programs. One of the most effective ways of implementing this theme is to have a senior officer address each training class to emphasize that ethical behavior is an imperative at all levels of the organization.

   Another approach is to have the instructor cite several examples of how employees have gone beyond the call of duty to do the right thing for customers and fellow workers. Such real-life stories become the folklore that inspires others to act in a similar fashion.

5. Develop and implement appraisal and reward systems that reflect the importance of ethics in decision-making. Remember, you get the behavior you reward.

6. In employee newsletters, praise the noteworthy ethical deeds that employees have done in their operations. This will help keep ethics at the forefront of everyone's mind.

7. Establish a mechanism for employees to report unethical behavior. One plan of action is to create a company ethics officer or ombudsman. Another is to have an "Ethics Violation Hotline." For any approach to be successful, anonymity must be guaranteed for those who report ethics violations.

8. Establish effective auditing systems to ensure that the organization's ethical values are adhered to. And of course, take strong corrective action whenever violations are discovered.

In summary, **having strong ethics is critically important for achieving career success.** The good news is that you can decide to live an ethical life if you are willing to make the personal commitment to do so and have the courage to stay the course. In addition, it's never too late to start. The important point is that the future is open. *It all depends on you!*

Chapter Ten

"E" Core Strategy Takeaways

1. The most important imperative for career success is being ethical in your business dealings—doing what is right, good, honest, and fair. This is what builds trust—the foundation of successful leadership.

2. Companies that have a reputation for being ethical have a greater chance of succeeding than those that do not.

3. Ethics is good for your soul and when your soul is healthy, so is your overall well-being.

4. Strong ethics helps establish and preserve your reputation.

5. The bottom line: it pays to be ethical.

6. If your organization asks you to do something that you believe is unethical, you should first make sure of the facts, and then refuse to act unethically.

7. Do not remain with an unethical organization. Go for long-term success by seeking employment with an organization that strives to be ethical.

8. Live your life by the highest ethical standards.

9. To live an ethical life you should:
   a) Make a personal commitment to do so.

b) Develop the habit of being ethical.
c) Emulate ethical leaders.
d) Surround yourself with ethical people.
e) Utilize the following Ethics Guideline Questions to help you determine the right thing to do.
   i. Is it legal?
   ii. Does it harm anyone?
   iii. Is it fair?
   iv. How would I like to be treated in a similar situation?
   v. Does my behavior reflect favorably on how I would like to be remembered?
   vi. Will I respect myself for what I did?
10. Set the example for others to follow by performing all your duties in an ethical manner.

Core Strategy #2:
"C" for Caring for Others

Chapter Eleven

What is a "Caring for Others" Spirit?

"The true measure of a man is how he treats someone who can do him absolutely no good."

—Samuel Johnson

The second value component of the ECL Core Strategy for Success is represented by the letter "C": Caring for Others. The concept of caring for others is a key factor in distinguishing an effective leader

> ECL Core Strategy:
>
> *"E" for Ethics*
> **"C" for Caring for Others**
> *"L" for Lifelong Learning*

from an average one. All other things being equal, people respond better to leaders who sincerely care for them. Loyalty, teamwork, and extra effort are all by-products of a "caring for others" environment stimulated by the person in charge.

The two key components of a "caring for others" spirit are: 1) *empathy*—the ability to identify with another's distress and to feel what it's like to be in his or her place and 2) *compassion*—to have sorrow for the sufferings and troubles of others. A leader with these wonderful human qualities tends to be kind, considerate, and most important, unselfish. An unselfish leader is generous in giving himself or herself to assist those who are less fortunate and unable to help themselves. The gifts of self usually involve elements of personal value such as love, time, knowledge/talents, or money.

> **Q:** *How do you know if you have a true "caring for others" spirit?*
> **A:** *If you strive to care for others in the same way that you care for yourself.*

True self-giving is unconditional in the sense that it does not depend on the giver's receiving anything in return. In other words, a person with a true "caring for others" spirit sets no conditions for the type of individual he or she helps, neither does the giver have to admire, like, or even approve of the recipient's behavior. Also, a "caring for others" spirit is totally blind to the race, color, creed, gender, age, ethnicity, nationality, or class of the recipient.

Contrast this "caring for others" spirit with that of a person motivated primarily by self-interest. As previously mentioned, "Selfish people look at the world as a 'give a little, take a lot' proposition in that they put their own agenda first."[21]

It's important that a "caring for others" spirit come naturally from the heart. This is necessary for it to be meaningful. You can't fake caring, as most people can quickly sense the level of sincerity of a person who offers to help.

Finally, having a "caring for others" spirit does not preclude a leader from being goals-orientated, aggressive, and strong-willed in his or her business dealings. All too often I've seen people initially assume that a leader with a good heart is soft or lacks competitive spirit. In most cases they were quickly proven wrong. A caring spirit is compatible with a bold, dynamic business approach.

Journalist and lecturer Gail Sheehy says, "In a capitalist system based on unbridled competition, we worry that if we care, we lose . . . compassion is thought of as being a woman's word . . . in men it's cast as wimpy, when in fact it makes us stronger under stress and more highly respected by our peers."[22]

> *It staggers me that being nice is seen as being inconsistent with being tough.*
>
> **Craig E. Weatherup**
> (Former C.E.O. of Pepsi Bottling Group)

A leader high in "C" can pursue organizational excellence as aggressively as anyone else. He or she can also be firm and hold people accountable. The difference is only in the approach. The leader with a "caring for others" spirit is more apt than the insensitive, self-centered leader to give thoughtful consideration in advance to the adverse impact decisions have on the employees affected by them. In addition, the "caring for others" leader handles the implementation of difficult personnel decisions in a far more compassionate manner.

Why does having such a "caring for others" spirit matter when making difficult personnel decisions? It matters because it helps preserve the reputation of the leader as always being a people-person. Employees are far more likely to cooperate when asked to do more with less when they realize their leader has a heart.

In the forthcoming chapter you will learn why competitive, strong-willed leaders who are also high in "C" have a distinct advantage in winning the loyalty and cooperation of their employees.

Chapter Twelve

Why Have a "Caring for Others" Spirit?

It is not enough merely to exist. It's not enough to say, I'm earning enough to support my family, I do my work well, and I'm a good father, husband, and church-goer. That's all very well. But, you must do something more. Seek always to do some good somewhere.

—Albert Schweitzer

There are several important reasons for having a "caring for others" spirit. The first one is related to why we exist. I believe that we as individuals were put on this Earth for a higher-order purpose than merely seeking to satisfy our personal needs and wants. Yes, these things are important, but not as important as the greater purpose of glorifying God and serving others.

The only way we can truly fulfill this higher-order purpose is to move beyond a me-first mentality that focuses on the accumulation of wealth and self-gratification to an others-first mentality. This opens our hearts and minds to feel empathy and compassion for people everywhere and inspires us to take appropriate action to help alleviate injustice, prejudice, and suffering wherever it exists. The end result of such a caring attitude is a better world for all of us.

Core Strategy for Success

In our day-to-day busyness with job and family, it's easy to overlook the fact that millions of people, even some in our own community, lack adequate food, shelter, health care, and educational opportunities. There are countless others who have debilitating illnesses and suffer from high levels of stress, anxiety, and loneliness. In short, the human needs everywhere are so great that it behooves everyone, especially leaders, to adopt a "caring for others" spirit and then do something tangible about fulfilling those needs.

The second reason for having a "caring for others" spirit is that it helps the leader be successful. In the "E" for Ethics chapter, it was highlighted that leadership success is all about building relationships through trust and that trust is fostered by the leader's demonstration of high ethical standards by doing what is right, good, honest, and fair.

> *Anytime we extend ourselves, sacrifice, and serve others, we build authority and thereby influence.*
>
> **James C. Hunter**
> (Leadership consultant and writer)

But, it takes more than just trust to create an inspired workforce. Employees must feel that their leader sincerely cares about them as individuals. What counts most is the attitude of the leader. If he or she demonstrates a "caring for others" attitude by listening carefully, unselfishly giving credit where it is due, helping people succeed, and most important, being fair, people will respond in a positive manner.

It's a "caring for others" spirit that enables the leader to successfully navigate the often difficult waters of aligning the individual's goals with those of the organization and vice versa. Alignment is not easily accomplished. It usually involves considerable discussion, compromise, and willingness to subordinate one's objectives to those of the team.

When the leader sets the example by having a "caring for others" attitude, everyone is encouraged to act in a similar fashion toward each other and customers. The result: improved performance in many areas such as increased teamwork, lower absenteeism/turnover, and higher customer retention rates.

> *People who are cared about return that care to others.*
>
> *For Your Improvement*

The bottom line is that when a leader is both ethical (high in "E") and has a "caring for others" spirit (high in "C"), he or she possesses two of the most important attributes necessary for success over the long haul.

Caring in a leadership situation starts with the leader learning the names, backgrounds, and aspirations of the people in his or her organization. But, as previously mentioned, it goes even further than this. Being a caring individual means being tuned in to what employees are experiencing and feeling and then doing everything possible to help them succeed.

For a leader's acts of caring to be genuine, they must come from the heart. A caring spirit cannot be manufactured for any other motivation such as enhancing one's reputation in the eyes of staff members. The right motivation is to care for others because it is the best thing for them and their loved ones. Most people can determine whether their leader is authentic in this respect.

The third reason for having a "caring for others" spirit is that it helps make your life meaningful and joy-filled. Abraham Lincoln said it best: "When I do good, I feel good." The nineteenth century American educator Booker T. Washington added, "If you want to lift yourself up, lift someone else." In effect, personal joy is a by-product of caring for others.

All of us need to work for something that is larger than ourselves. As Helen Keller said, "Many people have the wrong idea of what constitutes true happiness . . . it's not obtained through self-gratification, but through fidelity to a worthy purpose." Charles Handy, in *The Age of Paradox*, writes, "We get our deepest satisfaction from the fulfillment and growth and happiness of others." So if you want to find true joy in your life, serve others with a caring heart.

> *Caring for others, running the risk of feeling, and leaving an impact on people brings happiness.*
>
> **Harold Kusher**
> (Author)

Often, what people remember most fondly about their careers are not the times of significant achievement, but rather the moments they were involved in coaching individuals to be successful and developing positive working relationships with peers and customers.

In review, it's important to have a "caring for others" spirit, for the following reasons:

1. It helps make our world a better place to live in.
2. It's important for career success.
3. It's necessary to make life meaningful and joy-filled.

Therefore, having a "caring for others" spirit is an imperative for all leaders.

Chapter Thirteen

Ways to Demonstrate Caring

Live a life that makes a difference for good.

Realizing the importance of caring for others in your career, what are some of the ways to demonstrate such a spirit? Previously I mentioned that to care for someone is to give that person something of yourself that is of value. The key words here are "give" and "of value."

Let's now look at how you can share each of your valuable possessions—your love, your time, your knowledge/talent, or your money—with others to help improve their lives.

1. The gift of love and time. One of the best ways to share your love and time is to constantly look for ways of doing considerate, often seemingly little actions to help others cope with the trying situations they're facing. To be truly meaningful, such acts of kindness are done without expectation of reward or payback of any kind. When you help another person without expecting something in return, your gift becomes far more meaningful than any physical item that you might give. The simple fact that you went out of your way to personally help, creates a feeling of uplift in the recipient—a feeling of being appreciated, valued, and loved. Victor Hugo said it best, "The supreme happiness in life is the conviction that we are loved."

Earlier I mentioned that I had the opportunity to work for Frank Borman, the astronaut and president of Eastern Airlines. He had a strong "caring for others" spirit that came from his heart. He often went out of his way to give of himself to others without ever expecting a payback in return.

Years ago, after returning home from a business trip for Eastern, I was startled to find Borman's car parked in my driveway. To put this incident in perspective, I was just a low level manager in the company, and now one of America's most respected business leaders and hero of the American space program had unexpectedly come to visit my home. Obviously, I was shocked and concerned.

> *The best portion of a good man's life: his acts of kindness and love.*
>
> **William Wordsworth**
> (19th century poet)

As I opened the back door to our family room and peered inside, I felt my heart pounding and my knees shaking, for certainly something terrible had happened. I will never forget the image that greeted me: Frank Borman, the famous astronaut, sitting on our couch next to my three-year-old daughter, Cindy, whose leg was in a full plaster cast. She was recovering from a serious knee operation. Borman had brought her a teddy bear to cheer her up!

Now, many years have passed and that tattered teddy bear is still one of Cindy's most cherished possessions—"the teddy bear from the famous astronaut."

> *The great paradox of life: the more you give of yourself, the more you receive.*
>
> **Author Unknown**

What's so special about this seemingly small incident in life? It's special because a very prominent and busy leader gave of himself and his valuable time to personally deliver the gift. He could have just as easily given the teddy bear to me at the office saying, "Here's a gift for Cindy" or mailed it to her or even had his wife, Susan, drop it off at our home. But what did he do? He went out of his way to bring it himself.

Ironically, the same afternoon that Borman delivered the teddy bear to Cindy, an accident occurred at a construction site a few blocks from our house. While walking next to a building, a worker was struck on the head by a heavy stucco tile that slid off the roof. It caused severe wounds and a concussion. He was rushed to the hospital, received numerous stitches, and was later released to spend time at home to recuperate. A number of his co-workers sent cards and visited him. Yet, the one person who did not demonstrate his caring spirit was the construction supervisor, the injured man's boss. He never called or inquired about the welfare of his employee.

Just as Cindy will never forget Frank Borman's caring thoughtfulness, the construction worker struck by the tile will never forget his supervisor's insensitivity and lack of concern.

But, the story doesn't end here. Years have now passed since Frank Borman delivered the teddy bear to Cindy. During that time, I've told that story to many people to illustrate the power of caring—giving of yourself to others.

The point is that Frank Borman and other caring people will be remembered more for what they did to help others on a personal basis than for what they achieved in their careers.

Core Strategy for Success

> What we have done for
> ourselves alone dies with
> us. What we have done for
> others and the world
> remains and is immortal.
>
> **Albert Pine**
> (19th century author)

The impact of a small, seemingly insignificant act of kindness toward another human being can go far beyond just creating fond memories. It can literally set in motion a chain of events that leads to significant change for the better in our society.

Such was the case on a beautiful autumn day in Anderson, South Carolina, in 1964. According to Gary Smith, writing in *Sports Illustrated*, "It all started with a dirty, disheveled eighteen-year-old boy, named James Robert Kennedy, roaring down a hill on a grocery cart, screaming like a banshee . . . no one ever plays with him, for he can barely speak and never understands the rules . . . he can't read or write a word . . . he needs to be put away in some kind of institution, people keep telling his mother, because anything, anything at all, can happen out there on the margin."[23]

On that particular day, late in the afternoon, Kennedy's grocery cart transported him to the fringes of the McCants Junior High School football practice field. There he observed the team practicing and did his best to mimic the coaches' body language and commands. Eventually, his loud noises distracted the players to the point that assistant coach Harold Jones, whose role was to maintain order and discipline on the field, yelled, "Come over here, boy." At first Kennedy did not respond and did so only when lured with a bottle of soda.

What happened after that first encounter between Coach Jones and Kennedy was the start of what sportscaster Jim Nantz called "one of the most inspiring stories I've ever read."[24] Coach Jones, instead of reprimanding Kennedy in an effort to keep him away, befriended him. He allowed the boy to remain with him on the sidelines during practices and games and even let him do odd jobs during the school day. After some difficult times, the players and townspeople grew to appreciate Kennedy's loving, supportive spirit.

Sports Illustrated writer Gary Smith found out about the budding relationship between Coach Jones and Kennedy, who had been affectionately nicknamed "Radio" because it seemed he always had a transistor radio next to his ear. Smith decided to visit Anderson, South Carolina, to find out firsthand if what he heard was true. And in December 1996, he published an article in the magazine titled "Someone to Lean On."

One thing led to another, and in 2003, Columbia Pictures released the film *Radio* that chronicled the first few years of the close relationship between Coach Jones and "Radio" Kennedy.

What started as a simple act of kindness from one human being to another led to the *Sports Illustrated* article, the movie, and countless speaking engagements by Coach

> It's remarkable what can result from a simple act of caring.

Jones, all of which have brought world-wide attention to the special needs of people like James "Radio" Kennedy.

There is one additional twist to this fascinating story. Several years ago, Coach Jones and "Radio" Kennedy visited my church in Hilton Head, South Carolina, to address the congregation. After the presentation, one of the parishioners asked Jones, "What drove you to help the boy?" Jones than related an incident that occurred early in his life when he was delivering newspapers one morning before dawn. As he approached a house set in from the road, he heard noises coming from under the crawl space below the front porch. Dismounting from his bike he took a closer look. He was startled to find a young child in a wire enclosure. Afraid, Jones threw the paper on the porch and fled. Days passed before he said anything. Later, while reflecting upon why he didn't report the apparent child abuse incident earlier, he swore to himself that if he ever had another opportunity to help someone in serious need by acting in a courageous manner that he would do so *no matter what!*

2. The gift of knowledge/talents. The Frank Borman and Coach Jones stories illustrate the power of giving love and time unselfishly to others. What about the giving of your knowledge and talents?

A good example is what a good leader does when he or she spends extra effort to develop a high-potential employee, knowing full well that that person will be promoted out of the organization.

Why do it when the loss of a key employee could adversely affect the short-term performance of your team? The answer is that it's the right thing to do for both the organization and yourself. Accelerating the development of the high-potential employee is obviously the right choice to make for the organization because it helps ensure its long-term success.

Being an unselfish coach is also the best thing for you to do personally. Having a good track record in this important area will attract competent people to your team. In addition, your reputation as a top-notch developer of people will be recognized and will help you obtain your career objectives.

3. The gift of money. The third way of demonstrating your "caring for others" spirit is to unselfishly help others financially. This is often the hardest thing for people to do.

> *It is where a man spends his money that shows where his heart is.*
>
> **A. Edwin Keignin**

Recently, on a television show, Jon Huntsman, founder of the multibillion-dollar company Huntsman Chemical, was interviewed. After explaining how successful Huntsman had become, the interviewer asked Huntsman to relate what happened during the recession of 2000–2001 when his company was faced with bankruptcy. Huntsman described how his company suffered continuous losses and was nearly out of cash.

"What did you do then?" asked the interviewer.

"I went to our lead bank and asked for a $50 million loan," replied Huntsman. "Of course, the banker was interested in what we intended to do with the money and how we would secure it."

"And what was your response?" prodded the interviewer.

"I told him that we were going to use the money to fulfill the pledges that we had made to various charities."

"How did the banker react to such a startling statement?"

"I think it 'floored' him. He had never heard of such a thing, a large loan being used during a recession to make charitable donations rather than to invest in marketing or productivity enhancements."

Then Huntsman proceeded to make a stunning announcement. He intended to leave the world in the same manner in which he came into it—totally broke— by donating his entire fortune to cancer research and other worthwhile causes.

> *Since we're alive for such a short time, the things we accumulate are only temporary. What lives are the things we've done to help others.*

This was a special teachable moment for millions of viewers throughout the country.

4. The gift of spontaneous selflessness. There is one additional act of caring for others that goes beyond the giving of your love, time, knowledge/talents, or money. And that is going the extra mile to help someone, possibly even a stranger, on a spontaneous basis. The natural tendency of many people is to be cautious before coming to the aid of someone they don't know. This is understandable with all the crime and legal issues we have in our society.

However, there is something inspiring about people who instinctively give of themselves without becoming paralyzed with uncertainty or fear.

Wesley Autrey is one such person. What he did on Tuesday afternoon January 2, 2007, at a New York City subway station was almost beyond belief.

While standing on a subway platform, Autrey watched in horror as twenty-year-old Cameron Hollopeter fell off the platform between the tracks. Apparently suffering from a seizure, Cameron was unable to move. When Autrey saw the rapidly approaching train headlights in the tunnel, without hesitating, he jumped off the platform and shoved the disoriented student into the only space where they had a chance to survive—the shallow, grimy drainage trough between the tracks. There Audrey pinned Hollopeter in the trough by lying on top of him, face to face.

After the incident, Autrey confessed that he had no idea whether there was enough space for the train to pass over them safely. He told one newspaper reporter, "I couldn't just watch a train run over a man."[25] When the subway officials measured the depth of the space *between* the tracks, they were amazed to discover only about two feet of clearance from the train to the bottom of the trough, meaning that the train passed over the top of the two men by only one or two inches."[26]

Having an attitude of spontaneous selflessness doesn't necessarily mean putting your life on the line for others. This is an extreme example. What it does mean, however, is that your initial instinct when observing a person in difficulty is to find a way to help him or her.

In review, a "caring for others" spirit involves giving something of yourself to others that is valuable, such as your love, your time, your knowledge/talents, your money, or even your spontaneous assistance in a time of need.

The illustrations so far have focused on people sharing one of their "gifts" at a time. Certainly it's possible to share several "gifts" at the same time. It's far more unusual, however, to share them all simultaneously. This is exactly what occurred when Dr. Muni Tahzib, a Hoboken, New Jersey. pediatrician, decided to help the unfortunate victims of the worst humanitarian crisis in decades— the January 12, 2010, earthquake in Haiti.

> *Never believe that a few caring people can't change the world.*
>
> **Margaret Mead**
> (20th century cultural anthropologist)

When her offer of service was rebuffed by several international relief organizations due to her lack of extensive field experience, Tahzib utilized Facebook to quickly form a team of seventeen doctors, nurses, and technicians. In just a matter of days she and her team arrived in Port-au-Prince with a load of medical supplies, food, and water. There she became a part of an extraordinary volunteer relief effort that included thousands of people like Tahzib who dropped everything in their lives to respond to the crisis with their love, time, knowledge/talents, and money to help those in desperate need. As the title of the lead article in the February 28, 2010, issue of *Parade Magazine* boldly proclaimed, "This is What Being Human is all about."

Chapter Fourteen

How to Become a More "Caring for Others" Leader

"Call, visit, or write someone in need every day.

—Dennis Waitley

Now that you understand why it's important to have a "caring for others" spirit and have been exposed to some of the ways to demonstrate it, the question evolves into how a leader becomes more sensitive to the needs of others.

As mentioned earlier, a "caring for others" spirit can't be faked. For it to have a positive impact on others, the "spirit" must be sincere—it must come from the heart.

Most people have the capacity to enhance the "C" in their lives even if they haven't been fortunate enough to learn this trait early in life by emulating the behavior of respected adults, such as parents, relatives, teachers, and coaches.

If caring for others is not your strong suit, it's not too late to change for the better. As in acquiring any other positive behavior in life, you have to first make a commitment to change. Martin Luther King, Jr. said it best: "Every man must decide whether he will walk in the light of creative altruism or in the darkness of destructive selfishness."[27]

For many leaders, making such a commitment is difficult, especially if they're in the habit of frequently judging others. For such leaders to acquire a "caring for others" spirit they first must work at accepting people for who they are and not getting absorbed in negative thoughts about their inadequacies. A former colleague of mine once told me that all people are like round dowels with a flat side and that our role in life is to accept everyone despite their flat sides—inadequacies.

The practice of judging people in an effort to prove our own self-worth gets in the way of accepting others for who they are. If we can somehow overcome this tendency, we're able to move on to the next step in the process of acquiring a "caring for others" spirit.

> *Begin each day with the intent to help someone in need.*

This step involves practicing specific acts of caring to the point that you do them without even thinking about it. This is accomplished by pushing yourself to act in a compassionate manner time after time. Start by being on the lookout each and every day for ways to help others. John Wooden, one of the most successful college basketball coaches of all time, has a philosophy that every day he is supposed to help someone who can never reciprocate.[28]

If you open your eyes and heart to the concept of having a "caring for others" spirit, you will be amazed at the opportunities that await you for helping those who can't help themselves. The opportunities are everywhere if you just look! It may be as simple as assisting an elderly person struggling to cross a busy street before the light changes, holding the elevator for someone approaching in a wheelchair, offering to exchange seats with another passenger on an air-flight so a family can sit together, or providing encouraging words to a new employee who appears overly stressed.

Most people can relate to the experience of having been stuck in a long line at a store checkout counter because the cashier was obviously new to the job. When this happens to you again, view it as an opportunity to demonstrate a "caring for others" spirit by remaining calm and, if necessary, reminding the others in line about how they must have felt when they were a new employee. And when it's your time to check out, offer some kind words of encouragement to the trainee.

> *Too often we underestimate the power of a touch, a smile, a kind word, a listening ear, an honest compliment, or the smallest act of caring, all of which have the power to turn a life around.*
>
> **Leo F. Buscaglia**
> (20th century author)

At work, demonstrate a "caring for others" spirit to employees suffering from serious illness or grief over the loss of a loved one. Even if you have many people in your organization, set up a system that ensures you're notified about such happenings in a timely fashion. Then respond personally in an appropriate manner that demonstrates that you really do care.

For example, if a spouse of a staff member passes away, attend the funeral and express your heartfelt sympathy to the family. Or, if one of your associates is hospitalized, visit or phone the person. For employees further down in the organization who are hospitalized or suffering grief, send a card with a personal note. Whatever you do, avoid using e-mail or texting, even if the employee is located thousands of miles away. The point is that you *act in some appropriate manner* to help soothe the pain of the people you're responsible for. Your gesture of doing something tangible speaks louder than words. It says, "I care and appreciate you!"

Although the most important aspect is the willingness of the leader to give of himself or herself to others, it also matters a great deal how the "gifts" are delivered. For example, the "gift" of a leader's time and talent in coaching a subordinate is substantially depreciated if it is given in an insensitive or disrespectful manner.

Throughout the years I've seen this happen on a number of occasions. One day I overhead a manager severely berating an employee in the hallway for something she had done. Although the boss was giving her time in an effort to teach the person something, the approach was ineffective because it was so demeaning. I doubt the employee learned anything from the session except to dislike the boss even more.

"Caring for others" leaders act in certain ways that demonstrate that they truly value people. Some of these ways include the following:

- Listening attentively.
- Being respectful.
- Keeping promises.
- Insuring fairness and equity.
- Recognizing good work.
- Emphasizing personal growth and development.
- Subordinating self-interest to that of the organization and the employees.

Another way to become a more caring person is to open your senses to the people around you. When you observe a person who's obviously bearing a heavy burden, send that person a positive mental thought—what I call a positive "vibe."

Recently, on a visit to see family in central Illinois, I was picking up the *Wall Street Journal* at a drug store when I saw a man in a wheelchair making his way through the pelting sleet from the parking lot to the store entrance. I recall sending him the thought that "he'd continue to have the courage to endure his obviously difficult life." I'm convinced that there is considerable power in such positive "vibes." The more you do it, the more sensitive you'll become to the needs of others.

In short, you can enhance your "caring for others" spirit by making it a practice to think more of others and then acting to help those in need. If you consistently do this, it will not be long until unselfish, caring behavior becomes one of your strong suits.

In summary, **the best measure of a person's life is the positive influence that he or she had on the lives of others.** The positive impact comes from thinking of others as much as you do of yourself and from freely sharing your gifts of love, time, knowledge/talents, and money with those in need.

> *The big question for everyone: How will you live your life? Will you be a taker or a giver?*

Always remember that the "C" in the ECL Core Strategy for Success stands for having a "caring for others" spirit.

Chapter Fifteen

"C" Core Strategy Takeaways

1. The two key components of a "caring for others" spirit are
   a) *empathy*—the ability to identify with another person's distress and
   b) *compassion*—to have sorrow for the sufferings and troubles of others.
2. Having a "caring for others" spirit in your job does not preclude you from being goals-orientated and strong-willed.
3. It's important to have a "caring for others" spirit for the following reasons:
   a) It helps make our world a better place to live in.
   b) It's essential for career success.
   c) It's necessary to make life meaningful and joy-filled.
4. You can demonstrate a "caring for others" spirit in your career by giving something of yourself that is of value—your love, your time, your knowledge/talents, or your money.
5. "Caring for others" leaders act in certain ways that demonstrate that they truly value people. Some of these ways include listening attentively, being respectful, keeping promises, insuring fairness and equity, recognizing good work, emphasizing personal growth and development, and

subordinating self-interest to that of the organization and the people in it.

6. Most people have the capacity to become more caring if they do not already have this trait. It can be accomplished by developing the habit of constantly looking for opportunities to help others either directly or indirectly.

7. **The best measure of a person's life is the positive influence that he or she had on the lives of others.** And that positive influence comes from thinking of others as much as you do of yourself and from freely sharing of your gifts with those in need.

Core Strategy #3:
"L" for Lifelong Learning

Chapter Sixteen

The Importance of Lifelong Learning

"Live to learn and you will learn to live!"

—Portuguese Proverb

The third value component of the ECL Core Strategy for Success is represented by the letter "L" for Lifelong Learning—seeking to reach your highest career potential by having a passion for continuous self-development.

> ECL Core Strategy:
>
> *"E" for Ethics*
> *"C" for Caring for Others*
> **"L" for Lifelong Learning**

In today's highly competitive knowledge-based economy, being average (studying two or fewer hours per week) in the effort to develop yourself is a recipe for career mediocrity or even failure. Certainly, it will not enable you to reach your highest career potential.

Succeeding in today's world is extremely difficult, and it's going to become even more rigorous in the future because of the increasing velocity and complexity of change. The world of business will be more interconnected, more complicated, more unpredictable, and more competitive than ever before.

Core Strategy for Success

The fact is, we are living in the most competitive job market of all time, and it's only going to get more competitive in the future. In my generation, the competitors for the best jobs were people who obtained university degrees in the country where they were born and raised. But things are different today. Now, applicants for managerial positions include graduates from universities throughout the world— graduates who are highly motivated to improve their station in life.

Also, obtaining an MBA degree is no longer unique. According to the United States Department of Education, approximately 150,000 MBA degrees are awarded each year in this country. What this fact means is that you must have an MBA just to be on a level playing field with those that already do when seeking the best jobs.

> *Whatever made you successful in the past won't in the future.*
>
> **Lew Platt**
> (Former CEO of Hewlett Packard)

In addition, many mid-level jobs are either being eliminated or outsourced to countries with low wage costs. The result is that more and more highly educated people are competing for fewer and fewer good positions.

There is only one answer to this serious dilemma: no matter what your age or what level you achieve in your organization, **you must continue to grow and develop. You cannot afford to let up in any way.**

> *Control your destiny by taking full responsibility for your career development.*

All too often, leaders reach a certain plateau in their organizations and then begin to coast. They become sufficiently comfortable with their level of expertise and they assume they know all there is to know. The result: they stop striving to learn. Simultaneously, major advancements continue in their occupational fields, leaving the complacent learners obsolete in terms of their knowledge and skills. According to Jeffrey Schmidt, a managing director at Towers Perrin, "You have to assume that the half-life of the skill set you've got is about three to five years."[29]

So, if you're one of the many who have reached a coasting point in your desire to constantly improve, watch out. It won't be long until you're replaced by someone who has made the investment in time and energy to keep up-to-date.

The bottom line: the only job security you have today is your motivation and capacity to continually renew yourself.

Chapter Seventeen

Becoming Great

"Our greatness lies not so much in being able to remake the world . . . as in being able to remake ourselves."

—Mohandas K. Gandhi

Being a passionate lifelong learner can do more for you than just make you more competitive at work; it can also lead to greatness.

If you haven't read the article "What it Takes to be Great" in the October 2006 edition of *Fortune Magazine*, I strongly urge you to do so by looking it up online. In summary, it says that greatness in any walk of life is not reserved for the few who are born with high intelligence

> *The most exciting journey you will ever take: going from what you are today to what you are capable of becoming.*

or with perceived natural talent. Rather, **greatness comes to those who are motivated to continually improve themselves.**

Did you ever wonder how Warren Buffett became the most successful investor of all time? Recently, a reporter asked him this question and he responded by saying, "I just read . . . I read all day."[30] Buffett's good friend and co-founder of the Microsoft Corporation, Bill Gates, also covets knowledge. According to *Fortune*, "He spends just about every spare waking minute studying science texts, or watching university courses on DVDs."[31]

Warren Buffet, Bill Gates, and hundreds of other very successful people all hold the same belief: if you want to reach your highest potential in your career, make continuous self-development a major priority.

As the Accenture Corporation, a leader in consulting, technology, and outsourcing says in one of its magazine advertisements, "True high performers aren't defined by what they do to reach the top, but rather by what they do to stay there. It's what we call continuous renewal and it's one of our key findings from our proprietary research."[32]

But, even though this recipe for success—continuous renewal—is well known, I've noticed that a strange thing happens to most college graduates after they've been in the work force for fifteen to twenty years. They lose "the eye of the tiger" in terms of their passion to continually develop themselves. More than likely, they start their careers with excitement and enthusiasm to acquire new knowledge and skills as quickly as possible. But, as the years pass, they lose focus and their excitement for career development wanes.

> *The people who succeed are the few who have the ambition and willpower to develop themselves.*
>
> **Herbert Casson**
> (20th century journalist)

In the article, "What it Takes to be Great," *Fortune* reports a similar phenomenon: "In virtually every field of endeavor, most people learn quickly at first, then more slowly, and then stop developing completely."[33]

If you're just starting your career, the trick is to maintain your early enthusiasm for learning throughout your life. If you do so, you will have a strong competitive advantage for the better jobs.

> *Anyone who stops learning is old, whether at twenty or eighty. Anyone who keeps learning stays young.*
>
> **Henry Ford**
> (Founder of the Ford Motor Company)

For mid-career and even late-career people, it's not too late to get back in the learning groove of being a passionate learner. **At any point in your life you can remake yourself**—*if* you really want to.

In review, if your objective is to achieve success in your profession and possibly even reach greatness, you must have a passion for constantly learning and improving. This zest for learning must continue throughout your career both on and off the job.

Chapter Eighteen

How Do You Rate as a Lifelong Learner?

"Good enough is the enemy of excellence."

—Author unknown

In their study of top leaders in all fields, Warren Bennis and Burt Nanus found, "It is the capacity to develop and improve their skills that distinguishes leaders from their followers."[34] The researchers also came to the conclusion that "leaders are perpetual learners."[35]

> *Leadership and learning are indispensable to each other.*
>
> **John F. Kennedy**

Knowledge by itself will not make you a successful leader, but without it, you will not become one. The important point is that leaders have a thirst for constantly improving themselves through continuous learning. This learning can be from experience, observation, discussion, and self-study.

Most people, if queried, would say that they fit Bennis's and Nanus's description of being a perpetual learner. This is probably true for them at work where they're constantly exposed to change and the need to master the details of new products, services, and systems.

> *New career? Young kids? Trying to make new friends? Who has the time for regular career self-study at home? You do if you want to reach your highest career potential.*

At home, however, most people "go on vacation" when it comes to regularly studying for the purpose of enhancing their careers. While off work, they prefer to relax with family or friends, read, watch television, or surf the Internet. In effect, they become "self-development dropouts" during a significant portion of their careers.

To reinforce my point, spend a moment jotting down the average number of hours of personal time (off the job) that you normally devote each week studying to enhance your professional knowledge and skills. If your answer is two hours a week (equivalent to seventeen minutes a day) or less, you're in good company, for that's what the vast majority of people do.

The most frequently cited reason for not regularly spending more personal time preparing for future career opportunities is that the effort takes away from other interests. Such rationale is understandable. More often than not, if the "self-development drop-outs" were to analyze how they spend their discretionary time, they would be surprised to learn that with a slight adjustment in priorities, they could free sufficient time for considerable self-improvement study.

According to the "American Time Use Survey" released by the U.S. Department of Labor, the average American spends nearly three hours per day watching television.[36] Add in Internet time and it's even more. Most of this time is for the purpose of being entertained—not for sharpening business acumen or perfecting leadership skills.

The bottom line is that very few people are passionate enough about reaching their highest career potential to regularly invest time off the job to become more promotable. Herein is a tremendous opportunity—if you dare to be different. By making a slight adjustment in your priorities, you can free at least one and a half hours each day for self-development time, and thereby set yourself apart from everyone else.

Chapter Nineteen

Strategies for Being an Exceptional Lifelong Learner

"Knowledge is power."

—Sir Francis Bacon

There are two basic ways to approach your career development. The first one is to let events and circumstances push you in one direction after another without establishing and maintaining a set course toward an ultimate goal. It's almost akin to navigating the ocean without instruments. The second approach is to take responsibility for your development by establishing a plan for what you want to achieve in your career, and then diligently working your plan out by becoming an exceptional lifelong learner.

A number of strategies can be utilized in the effort to become an outstanding lifelong learner. The two that stand out involve career planning and self-study. Although these strategies are known to produce excellent results, few people are willing to adopt them because of the extra effort that is required.

The critical questions to ask yourself are:

- do you really want to reach your highest career potential and if so,
- are you willing to make the necessary investment in time and energy to do so?

An affirmative answer to these questions means you're ready to consider how best to utilize the strategies described on the following pages.

Lifelong Learning Strategy #1: Prepare a Career Development Plan. Formal career developmental planning has long been utilized by well-run organizations to enhance long-term performance. However, few individuals use this approach to facilitate their own careers.

The overall purpose of a Career Development Plan is to help you add value to your work for your current employer while simultaneously preparing to achieve your ultimate career objective(s).

There are two important steps to take in creating a Career Development Plan. The first is to visualize what you want to achieve in your career. This is your dream for the future. The second step involves developing specific strategies and objectives for making your vision a reality.

> Reach high, for stars lie hidden in your soul.
> Dream deep, for every dream precedes the goal.
>
> **Pamela Vaull Starr**
> (20th century poet)

Career Development Plan Step #1: Create a vision of what you want to achieve in your career.

In his book, *The Richest Man Who Ever Lived—King Solomon's Secrets to Success, Wealth, and Happiness*, Steven K. Scott makes a strong case for having a well-defined vision in your professional life. He says, "Without a vision, our innermost being begins to waste away . . . the joy of living is replaced with the mere act of surviving or 'just getting by' . . . you go from joy to subsistence to depression and ultimately to despair."

Nothing is more conducive to career success than locking on to a specific overall vision of what you want to accomplish and then pursuing it with all your might. All the very successful people I've known have this "laser-like" focus. They seem to thrive on the challenge of striving for an overall career objective and, more importantly, they never submit to failure. They just don't quit! They may experience setbacks or even failures from time to time, but they view difficult experiences as opportunities to further grow and develop. In addition, there's something quite magnetic about people who know where they're headed in life. Good feelings and positive energy radiate from such people. In short, they become attractive candidates for promotional opportunities on the way toward their ultimate career objective.

Although most people intuitively know how important it is to have direction in their lives, few of them take the time to develop a definitive vision of what they want to achieve. Absent an end-goal, they often

> It's never too early to start thinking about where you want to end up.
>
> (Movie: *The Big Kahuna*)

appear to be rudderless, wondering from one job assignment to another and taking whatever training opportunities are offered by their employers.

Your vision statement should be bold in nature and take into account your dreams of what you want to achieve in your career. It should be both challenging and realistic. Finally, it should be brief, hopefully only one sentence in length. For

example, your vision statement could be as simple as, "By age
___ I want to be _____."

To facilitate the identification of your initial career vision or help you change an existing one, it's helpful to utilize the following four-step analytical approach:

1. The starting point in creating a vision statement is to ask yourself, "What do I really want out of life?"
2. Determine what you're most interested in doing— what you seem to constantly be drawn to. It cannot be stressed strongly enough how important it is to be employed in a field that you truly enjoy. It has been shown time and time again that people who are stimulated and challenged by their work are far more successful and happier than those who find it boring and tedious.
3. Identify your core competencies—those competencies in which you excel. These are your gifts in life. Ideally, your gifts are important for success in the occupational area you're interested in. For example, being good at debating would be a definite asset if you're considering being a lawyer.
4. Identify organizations that have a need for your gifts. An added plus would

> *Seek a profession of service and contribution.*

be if you can work in a field that makes a positive impact on the lives of others. Besides the education, medical, legal, and public service sectors, many businesses have a direct impact on making the world a better place to live in. There is a definite feeling of well-being and fulfillment when a person's occupation directly adds value to the world or serves a greater cause or purpose than merely maximizing profitability.

As newscaster Barbara Walters says, "Personal gain is empty if you do not feel you have positively touched another's life." So if you're able to have a career that's enjoyable and also utilizes your talents to make life better for others, you're blessed indeed!

It's obviously better to establish your career vision early in life, but it's never too late to do so. For many people, their ultimate life-dream is a constant work in progress until the end-goal is achieved. Some noteworthy examples of late bloomers include Colonel Sanders, Anna Mary Robertson, and Sylvia Lieberman. Colonel Sanders started his restaurant franchise business when he was sixty-five. Anna Mary Robertson ("Grandma Moses") taught herself to paint when she was in her seventies and later became famous throughout the world for her folksy style of art. And Sylvia Lieberman at age ninety became an entrepreneur by starting the company Archibald Mouse Books to promote her books that teach children how to achieve their big dreams.

> *Dream! Dream! And then go for it!*
>
> **Desmond Tutu–** (20th century South African cleric and activist)

Of course, it's always appropriate to inject a dose of reality into the determination of what you want to achieve in life, especially if you have a serious physical or mental limitation. Still, the principle holds that you can aspire to be about anything you want in life if you really apply yourself and make good choices along the way. Your dream can become reality!

Career Development Plan Step #2: Develop strategies and objectives for reaching your career vision. This involves answering such questions as these:

- What key areas of expertise are necessary for success as I have defined it?
- What educational level/professional certification is required?
- What sequence of jobs best prepares me for my end goal?
- What additional training experiences would add to my qualifications?
- Who best can mentor me along the way?
- What personal developmental activities (off the job) best prepare me to reach my vision of what I eventually want to be?

Your Career Development Plan should be in writing to facilitate clarity of thinking and organization. Most people take their written commitments far more seriously than their verbal ones.

At least once a year, it's helpful to review your vision and plan and make appropriate adjustments. Cultural anthropologist Mary Catherine Bateson says, "Our children are unlikely to be able to define their goals and then live happily ever after . . . instead, they will need to reinvent themselves again and again in response to a changing environment."

For example, you may have changed employers or even decided to undertake a new career field. Certain obstacles may have arisen such as health or family issues that affect your ability to focus on self-study. After factoring in the changes, rethink your strategic approach to make sure it leads you toward your dream. Finally, assess the extent of your motivation to develop yourself. Are you still willing to make the necessary sacrifices to study on a continuous basis?

New Year's Day or shortly thereafter is an excellent time to conduct such a review since most people feel a strong sense of new beginnings at that time. With "the promise of better things to come," rededicate yourself to meet the commitments in your plan.

In review, the first key strategy for becoming a lifelong learner is to prepare a career development plan that includes your vision of what you want to be in life and specific strategies and objectives for achieving it. The second key strategy is to study extensively.

Lifelong Learning Strategy #2: Study Extensively. Without question, the best way to facilitate the achievement of your career vision is to adopt an *extensive* and *focused* self-study program during your personal

> *Read every day something no one else is reading.*
>
> **Christopher Morley**
> (20th century novelist)

time. The words "extensive" and "focused" are italicized on purpose, for they are the critical drivers of this highly effective developmental activity. "Extensive" does not mean a little sporadic study from time to time, but rather a dedicated effort to study at least an hour and half a day, week after week, and year after year. By "focused" study I mean selecting articles, books, CDs, and DVDs that best help you meet your goals. The Internet also offers a wide variety of focused educational opportunities.

The most effective approach is to focus on developing the knowledge and skills identified in your Career Development Plan. For example, if you're weak in managerial finance and if knowledge of this discipline is important for achieving one of your targeted job objectives, you should focus a considerable portion of your off-the-job study in this area. The same is true for any other functional area where you have a weakness.

The idea is to continuously educate and re-educate yourself, not only to stay current in your present area of responsibility, but also to acquire the necessary knowledge and skills required for the targeted positions in your Career Development Plan.

You may have seen the magazine and television ads that proclaim "Read to lead," or heard the phrase "Today a reader, tomorrow a leader." Although these catchy statements focus on only one medium—reading—they also apply to learning from CDs and DVDs.

Anne Fisher, a columnist for *Fortune Magazine*, says, "Regardless of your job, and no matter how low on the corporate ladder it is, get your hands on as many trade and business publications as possible and read, read, read." She adds, "If you learn the jargon, the trends, and the rules of the game, you'll become an expert; and experts make more money and get more promotions."[37]

> The secret of success in life is for a man to be ready for his time when it comes.
>
> **Benjamin Disraeli**
> (19th century British Prime Minister)

Increasing your industry and general business knowledge by studying extensively is an excellent way for you to become an "idea" person in your organization. Today, there's a premium on such people, as they're viewed as being extremely beneficial in helping organizations succeed in our highly competitive global economy.

Besides making yourself more valuable to your employer, extensive and varied self-study has the added benefit of making you a more interesting person to associate with. Although seldom talked about in the world of business, comfort level is one of the important subjective elements considered in determining who is or isn't promoted.

The best advice I ever received in this area was given to me in a training program that I attended shortly after becoming a first-level manager. The program discussion leader said, "If you want to get ahead in your career, read what the top people read—the *Wall Street Journal* and *Fortune* magazine."

I can recall asking him why he selected those journals. His response went something like this: "Because the *Journal* is the most comprehensive daily publication for keeping informed about current business developments and trends and *Fortune* is the best periodical for learning about business strategies." He continued by saying, "If you want to reach the top, you have to understand the trends in your field and think strategically . . . the best way to do so is to immerse yourself in the details of what outstanding business leaders and entrepreneurs are thinking and doing."

There's one additional benefit from extensive, focused self-study—it broadens your leadership skills. From biographies and autobiographies, you can learn from the experiences of other successful leaders, particularly the obstacles they faced and how they overcame them. These insights will be helpful in guiding your actions when you're faced with similar challenges.

Your self-development study time should be split approximately three ways: 1) information that will keep you apprised of developments and trends in your occupational field, 2) general business material to obtain ideas and spot new trends, and 3) biographical and autobiographical content about accomplished leaders to provide leadership insights and stimulate creative thinking.

Start by reading extensively in your field. Keep up to date by subscribing to the most comprehensive journals available. Supplement your industry reading by joining the leading national/international association in your field and attending at least one of their primary conferences each year. The idea is to become thoroughly knowledgeable about industry trends so you can effectively participate in strategic discussions during company meetings.

In addition, read several national newspapers (or the electronic equivalents) each day and several developmental books a month. If you do all this and take notes to enhance your retention, you will put yourself into the rare classification of being a dedicated lifelong learner. Remember, the most knowledgeable people have a decided advantage when competing for promotions at work.

I can imagine what many of you must be thinking at this point: "How in the world am I going to find the time to do all that self-study at home when I have to put in so many extra hours at work plus spend time with my loved ones?" This is a valid concern. However, I'm convinced that most people can carve out an average of one and a half hours every day for developmental study and still be an outstanding performer at work *and* have a meaningful personal life. Here are some practical suggestions for doing so:

1. **Get up a little earlier each morning** (e.g., 5:30 AM instead of 6:00 AM) and in the quiet of your household, read the print or electronic versions of the *Wall Street Journal* and the business sections of *USA Today* and/or *The New York Times*. In most areas of the country, you can have these national newspapers delivered to your

doorstep prior to 6 am. However, it may be more convenient to subscribe to the online versions of these publications.

If you elect not to subscribe to either the hard copy or electronic versions of the national newspapers, there is an alternative (and a free one at that) for keeping current of the latest business developments and trends: the Web site www.cnn.com. Use the "home" page to get a feel for the top world and national news and then go to the "Money" tab at the top of the page for all kinds of breaking business news stories. If you're pressed for time before you leave for work, at least skim the feature articles and scan for items of interest that might apply to your job. The idea is to start your job each day fully briefed on the major political, economic, and business developments that might affect your work. If you take the time to do so, you'll be as topical and current as any other executive in your company. In addition, you'll be an interesting person to associate with.

2. **Listen to instructional CDs** while traveling to and from work and on business trips.

3. **Reduce the time you watch television** for strictly entertainment purposes and/or pre-record your favorite shows to view them later without the commercials. For many channels, at least 25 percent of the airtime is devoted to advertising. If you don't pre-record, at least log in some

> *The average American will watch a full year's worth of commercials in his or her lifetime. Why not invest this year in something that really counts?*

productive study time during the frequent two or three-minute commercials on the network shows.

To illustrate the power of these approaches, let's assume that your television viewing time is equal to the national norm of three hours per day. This includes weekend viewing. Utilizing portions of the time saved from reducing viewing time, pre-recording selected programs, and studying during the ads, it would not be too difficult to free one hour per day for self-study.

4. **Read for self-development** purposes at lunch time if you're alone. Never waste this precious opportunity to learn.

5. **Utilize a handheld electronic device** to read or listen to instructional material whenever you have a few spare moments such as when traveling. I've noticed that few career people take advantage of such dead time to improve their knowledge and skills. Usually they focus on doing job related work leaving little or no time for self-development. Of course, you should give top priority to job matters, but always try to utilize a portion of your travel time for preparing for a brighter future.

Hopefully by now you're convinced that you can find the necessary personal time to focus on self-development and thereby be unique in this vitally important area.

By applying some combination of the previously mentioned strategies, here is how you can easily carve out one and a half hours per day for self-study"

- A half hour by getting up earlier each morning and studying.
- One hour a night by cutting back on television/Internet viewing time that is done strictly for pleasure and/or converting television advertising time to self-development time.
- A half hour by reading at lunch or during unproductive wait time away from the office.
- A half hour by listening to instructional CDs while traveling to and from work and on business trips.

Because of pressing job and/or family issues, it may be difficult to consistently study one and a half hours every day. So, if you're overly busy on certain work days and can't find time to study, you could

> *Each and every day dedicate yourself to learning as much as possible.*

make up for the lost time while traveling on business or during the weekend. However you accomplish the objective, the trick is to be consistent in terms of how many hours you study on a weekly basis.

If you meet the criterion of being a passionate lifelong learner (i.e., studying an average of one and a half hours per day), you'll be amazed at the results in terms of the increased depth and breadth of your business acumen. Remember, knowledge leads to good developments in your career.

Logging in a substantial number of study hours each week is only half the battle in learning. The other half is having a high retention rate. One of the best ways to retain material is to highlight "key learning points" in your readings and save them for future reference.

Another effective approach for increasing your retention rate is to take notes whenever you're involved in a learning situation. Although note-taking is commonly practiced by students while in college, few people seem to carry over this highly effective learning habit into later life. Check this out for yourself the next time you attend a seminar or training program in your field. You'll be surprised at how few people make the effort to record new insights and ideas.

Note-taking helps you retain information by keeping you active in the learning process. You're linking the new information to what you already know and creating a deeper understanding of the concepts. In addition, you will ask better questions in the question-and-answer periods.

In review, if you want to learn more, adopt productive learning habits. Stephen Covey, writing in *The 7 Habits of Highly Successful People,* says, "People who acquire productive habits are far more likely to be successful than those who acquire unproductive habits." As previously indicated, the two most productive self-study learning habits are: 1) focused study and 2) consistent study.

Other Effective Lifelong Learning Strategies: Besides creating a career development plan and devoting a set portion of your personal time each day for self-study, there are several other excellent learning approaches that can be adopted to facilitate your lifelong learning:

A. *Be a student of "leaders in action."* Make it a practice to carefully observe outstanding leaders as they perform their duties. Notice how they articulate a vision of the future and how they inspire others to achieve it. Observe how a leader's actions are perceived by others. Be a scholar of non-verbal behavior. In addition, identify the values and principles upon which outstanding leaders make decisions. Most important of all, adopt the approaches that involve treating people with respect and dignity and doing what is right, good, honest, and fair.

You can also learn by observing poor leaders in action. Notice how team members react to their leadership styles. Ask yourself if you would have used the same approach and, if not, what would you have done differently?

> *Learn from the best, and then add your own personal flair.*

Whenever possible, spend time with successful people. Be prepared to have conversations with them on a variety of current topics. Just by being with them you'll pick up valuable insights that will make you a better leader. Tim Conner, a leadership author and speaker, says, "You can cut twenty years off the learning curve by hanging around people who have done what you want to do."

There are three keys to effective learning from conversations with others. First, keep an open mind about what is being said. Second, listen intently. Third, ask questions for clarification and to draw out the other person. If you do all of the above, you'll be surprised at how much you learn.

B. *Make it a priority to keep abreast of emerging technology.* The best way to understand new technologies and their business potential is to actually use the new hardware and software when they're first introduced. For example, if you're not already using a smart phone for texting, remote e-mailing, and video messaging, begin to do so. In addition, learn how webinars (web conferences) and wikis (web pages that people can edit together) can enhance communication with associates in different locations.

There are a few ways to keep up with technology so you don't get stressed of feel left behind. Look at an area you want to know more about and focus on that technology with a friend who is already competent using it. Before you purchase a new electronic device write down the features you would use. Talk with friends and colleagues to get them to explain why they picked a certain model and what they like about it. Remember, technology is rapidly changing. Your role is as a lifelong learner is to keep informed about it.

Finally, get comfortable with the latest approaches for networking socially by creating a personal profile with "connections" on both LinkedIn and Facebook. Such experiential learning will not only enhance your ability to visualize creative applications in your business, it will also help you to maintain a modern image. In today's rapidly changing workplace, you can ill afford to appear inflexible and outdated at any age.

C. *Become involved in civic and community activities where you can practice servant leadership.* Valuable leadership lessons can be learned as you lead groups of volunteers or coach youth sports teams. In volunteer work the people you lead are not paid and therefore, have no obligation to do what you say. In order to be successful, you must be able to influence them to cooperate. It's far better to learn how to do this in a "safe" environment where your mistakes do not adversely affect your career.

D. *Maintain a Personal Success Journal* to help you in your lifelong journey to reach your highest leadership potential. For convenience and ease of updating, your journal should be in an electronic format. At a minimum it should include the following sections:

   a. Key concepts learned from self-study.
   b. Observations of "Leaders in Action."
   c. Reflections on your successes and failures and what you learned from them.

- The major benefit of keeping a Personal Success Journal is that it facilitates introspective learning. According to Harriette Cole in *Choosing Truth*, "Journaling helps unlock the treasures of wisdom and clarity that reside within all of us . For example, when tackling difficult tasks involving working with others, you may be

> *Life isn't about finding yourself—life is about creating yourself.*
>
> **George Bernard Shaw**
> (20th century playright)

confronted with reactions you did not expect. You may even be criticized for the way you handled a particular situation. Use your Personal Success Journal to help you think through what happened and how you might have responded in a better way. Try to determine whether the criticism fits a pattern with other input that you've received in the past. What, if any, behavioral change(s) should you consider making?

- Some people even keep a list of the good things that happen to them. Those who practice this habit say it helps them keep going during difficult times.

- Journaling is best accomplished when you can take a few moments each day to reflect in a quiet setting such as early in the morning or just before going to bed.

E. *Stick with your Career Development Plan.* All too often, people start such a program with the intention of seeing it through to the end. But somewhere along the line it gets deferred and then eventually abandoned. The rationale for quitting often goes something like this: "I was just

> None of the secrets of success will work unless you do.

too busy working" or "I didn't want to take away from family time." Certainly these are reasonable considerations, but more often than not, the person involved really doesn't have the motivation to do what is necessary to reach his or her highest potential. As mentioned earlier, **what distinguishes successful people from those who are not is the capacity and motivation to continually develop**

their knowledge and skills. The fact is, there's always time to work on improving yourself if you really want to. All it takes is the courage to start and the discipline to keep going.

Most people have the courage to undertake a strategy of becoming a lifelong learner. But few people have the self-discipline required to continue it day after day and year after year. Since repetitive behavior is the key to establishing a positive new habit, I strongly urge you to undertake a "thirty-day trial

> *Your own resolution to succeed is more important than any other thing.*
>
> **Abraham Lincoln**

self-study program." Since big changes often start with small steps, start slowly in your self-study program. For example, you may want to initially devote only fifteen to twenty minutes per day to it. Gradually work up to the recommended hour and one-half. By the end of your thirty-day trial program, your new study habits will become well engrained in your lifestyle. And best of all, you'll begin to see some positive results from your efforts such as being able to contribute more effectively at work and being a more interesting person. Hopefully, by the end of the trial period, these and other benefits will be so compelling that you will not want to abandon the study effort.

In review, you can greatly enhance your chances of reaching your highest career potential by being passionate about your self-development. True lifelong learners have this attitude.

Core Strategy for Success

If the idea of constantly working on your development seems a bit overwhelming at this point in your career, remember the answer to the question: How does one go about eating an elephant? *One bite at a time!*

> *Great things are not done by impulse but by a series of small things brought together.*
>
> **Vincent Van Gogh**

Achieving your highest career potential is much like the famous Green Bay Packers' football coach Vince Lombardi's definition of the game: "Football is a game of inches." The Chinese have another way of defining the same concept: "A journey of a thousand miles begins with a single step." So, approach the future with a vision of what you want it to be. **Think of it often; and steadily, ever so steadily, work to make it happen by taking one small developmental step at a time.** You will succeed if you approach your career in this fashion.

Remember, the "L" in the Core Strategy for Success represents Lifelong Learning—not just ordinary, casual learning, but extensive, focused, and introspective learning to continually grow and evolve professionally.

Chapter Twenty

"L" Core Strategy Takeaways

1. No matter what level you achieve in your organization, it's imperative that you continue to grow and develop.

2. "It is the capacity to develop and improve their skills that distinguishes leaders from their followers"— Warren Bennis.

3. We're living in the most competitive job market of all time, and it's only going to get more competitive in the future.

4. The only job security people have today is their motivation and capacity to continually update their knowledge and skills.

5. Few people are passionate enough about reaching their highest career potential to regularly invest time off the job to become more promotable. Herein is a tremendous opportunity, if you dare to be different. By regularly investing one and a half hours of your personal time each day, you can set yourself apart from everyone else.

6. Being a passionate lifelong learner can do more for you than just make you more competitive at work— it can also lead to greatness.

7. Greatness comes to those motivated to constantly learn more and more.

8. Key strategies for being an exceptional lifelong learner:
    - Prepare a Career Development Plan.
    - Study extensively (e.g., one and a half hours per day).
    - Be a student of "Leaders in Action."
    - Undertake extracurricular leadership development activities.
    - Maintain a Personal Success Journal.
    - Stick with your Career Development Plan.

The "Z" Word:
The Attitude
That Makes It All Happen

Chapter Twenty-One

Zeal

"Every great and commanding moment in the annals of the world is the triumph of some enthusiasm."

—Ralph Waldo Emerson

To make the ECL Core Strategy for Success work for you, it's necessary to have a proper attitude: Zeal (the "Z" word). Zeal means having intense enthusiasm for an ideal you believe in. Zeal is the driving force that enables you to integrate the ECL principles into your life—to live ethically, to have a "caring for others" spirit, and to be a passionate lifelong learner. Without zeal, little is achieved in any of these areas.

> *Experience shows that success is due less to ability than to zeal. The winner is he who gives himself to his work, body and soul.*
>
> **Charles Buxton**
> (19th century member of Parliament, and philanthropist)

There is one other important application of zeal that is necessary for career success. This involves having zeal for one's profession. Why is this so important? Because, all other things being equal, people who love their work perform better than those who find their jobs tedious, boring, and even stressful.

According to Richard J. Leider, writing in *The Power of Purpose*, "When the work we do is a mismatch with what we need and enjoy in basic ways, the mental and physical costs can be high . . . problems in performance can result, advancement is not likely, and personal frustration and stress can be wearing." In their book, *Success Built to Last*, Jerry Porras, Stewart Emery, and Mark Thompson go even further by saying, "It's dangerous not to do what you love . . . the harsh truth is that if you don't love what you're doing, you'll lose to someone who does!"

One day after my Dad retired, we were talking about his career, and he told me something I'll never forget. He said, "Sometimes when I was working I felt I'd be willing to pay the company for the privilege of just doing my job." This sounded strange to me at the time, but later, when I experienced the same joy in my work, I understood what he meant. What Dad was saying was that the challenge and excitement of his duties as a senior executive at the National Gypsum Company were so enjoyable that he'd do them for their own sake.

> *Enthusiasm (zeal) is the greatest asset—more than power or influence or money.*
>
> **Author Unknown**

Now, I'm sure that my father wouldn't have worked for free for very long because he had a family to support, but it was just his way of emphasizing how much he loved his job. The point is that he'd never have risen as far as he did in his career unless he truly enjoyed his work.

Having zeal for your work means you'd rather do it than almost anything else. It also means that you lose track of time when you do it.

When people are zealous about their work, they give heart and soul to it. Someone who's blessed in this way will know more and perform better than someone who dislikes what he or she does for a living.

Chapter Twenty-Two

Attributes of a Person with Zeal for Work

"Put your heart, mind, intellect, and soul even to your smallest acts. This is the secret of success."

—Sivananda Saraswati

It has been my experience that people who have zeal for their work have several attributes in common. First, they have a *positive attitude* about everything in their lives. And this positive attitude serves them well in their careers.

As my son-in-law Joe Akers is fond of saying, "Your attitude is your altitude." This means that you will go about as far in life as your attitude dictates. According to Joe Vitale, PhD, writing in *Bottom Line Personal*, "People who have positive thoughts about their careers are more likely to attract promotions and raises than those who think of their work as an unpleasant chore."

> *If you love your work, you'll be out there every day trying to do it the best you possibly can, and soon every-body around you will catch the passion from you like a fever.*
>
> **Sam Walton**
> (Founder of Wal-Mart)

Positive people tend to be hope-filled and have a "can do" spirit. They view their problems as challenges to overcome and believe that with every obstacle there is opportunity; you just have to search hard enough for it.

Take a moment to think about all the people you know who have a positive nature. Then look at what they've accomplished. There is a direct correlation—positive people tend to be the winners in life. They're the ones who make things happen.

In David Aikman's book, *Great Souls: Six Who Changed the Century,* he concludes that it was the attitudes of Billy Graham, Nelson Mandela, Aleksandr Solzhenitsyn, Pope John Paul II, Elie Wiesel, and Mother Teresa that set them apart from everyone else during their lives.[38] Each of these great souls rose above his or her circumstances and was known for having a positive attitude.[39]

Just as success comes to those who constantly hold positive mental images in their minds, failure comes to those who are preoccupied with negative thoughts. The latter has become known as the "Wallenda Factor." In 1978 while traversing a high wire in downtown San Juan, Puerto Rico, the famous aerialist Karl Wallenda fell to his death. Later his wife told reporters that her husband was

> *Nothing can stop the man with the right mental attitude from achieving his goal; nothing on Earth can help the man with the wrong mental attitude.*
>
> **W. W. Ziege**

obsessed with the feeling that he would fall. "All Karl thought about for three straight months prior to it was falling."[40] He was so concerned about his safety that he personally supervised the installation of the tightrope—something he had never done before.[41] By focusing on the negative, Wallenda lost his concentration and made a fatal mistake.

The second attribute of people who have zeal for their work is that they are extremely *focused*. History has demonstrated that those who made the greatest impact on improving the quality of life for others have been totally focused on their mission. One such person who immediately comes to mind is Dr. Martin Luther King Jr., who led the Civil Rights Movement of the 1960s. Another person further back in history that stands out is the Apostle Paul who led the effort to spread Christianity throughout the Roman Empire. Despite being repeatedly arrested, beaten, slandered, maligned, and persecuted, Paul never lost focus on his mission.

Some recent examples of highly focused leaders who have favorably impacted the lives of others include Bill Gates, the co-founder of Microsoft and the Bill and Melinda Gates Foundation, and Oprah Winfrey. Much of their success stems from their passion or zeal for fulfilling their missions.

> *Here is a simple but powerful rule: always give people more than they expect to get.*
>
> **Nelson Boswell**
> (18th century British writer)

Finally, people with zeal for their work *do more than what is required* of them. They always give their very best. In short, they create extra value by exceeding the expectations of their managers and customers.

As Apolo Ohno, the most decorated American winter Olympian of all-time says, "Before you go to bed every night ask yourself one single question: did you do everything you could today to make sure you did your very best?"

Chapter Twenty-Three

Finding Your Dream Job

"Aim at the sun, and you may not reach it; but your arrow will fly far higher than if you aimed at an object on a level with yourself."

—F. Howse

The important lesson for people considering what they want to do in their lives is this: seek work that you truly enjoy. Start by asking yourself what you would do if money weren't an issue.

Most people find their dream job by doing two things: 1) establishing a high-performance reputation and 2) networking extensively.

> *You cannot kindle a fire in any other heart until its burning within your own.*
>
> **Eleanor Doan**
> (Author and educator)

Nothing trumps your track record in creating future job opportunities. But, your performance reputation must extend beyond being considered competent and reliable. In addition, it's important to be known for having one or more unique capabilities such as being a creative problem-solver, a strategic thinker, or a performance turnaround specialist. Look for opportunities where you can demonstrate such skills. Also, do not neglect the importance of looking and acting like someone on the way up. Outplacements specialists Lester Minsuk and Phillis Macklin advise clients to dress like their boss's boss.[42]

Unfortunately, in today's "dog-eat-dog" business world, being a high performer is often not enough to ensure continuity of employment. You need an extensive network of quality business and social contacts to help you should you become a causality of a merger, downsizing, or a policy disagreement with your boss. Throughout your career, make it a priority to cultivate strong relationships with the influential people you work with and then stay in touch with them if you or they change employers.

In addition, join an active professional organization. This will serve the dual purpose of helping keep up-to-date in your field and providing an ideal way to network outside your company.

> Networking is everything in job searches.

It has been my experience that managers and executives often discount the value of becoming active in professional and trade organizations as a means of networking within their industry. This is a serious mistake as a high percentage of mid-level and upper-level jobs are secured from personal contacts outside your firm.

Don't limit yourself to just networking at work and in professional organizations. Apply the same approaches in social networking. Some great places to network off the job are in places of worship and in community work. Also, don't miss the opportunity to network while watching your kids play sports or participate in other school activities.

Besides networking in person, do so online. Establish your personal profile on social sites such as LinkedIn that are used extensively by company recruiters and search firms to find professionals, managers, and executives. The value of a site such as LinkedIn is that people can leverage their networking far beyond what they can do by handing out business cards and making personal contacts. This is because you can use the Web site to join various kinds of affinity clubs such as one for your university, industry, and interest area(s). The networking leverage comes from linking these groups to your personal profile.

Social sites also enable you to network without appearing to be shopping for a new job. Even if you're not looking, it's advisable to keep your profile current and to join various groups since most corporate recruiters and "head hunters" prefer to look at candidates who are currently employed. You never know when a more exciting job opportunity might come your way.

In all your networking activities, have a strategy for what you want to accomplish. Determine in advance those who might be helpful to you in your career, and then find ways to meet and get to know them. Offer to help them without implying that you expect anything in return. If you maintain this attitude, you will not be guilty of using them strictly for your own benefit. Remember that life has a way of paying back those who help others.

As a side note, never "burn your bridges" when leaving an employer for any reason. Even if you're terminated, don't leave in a huff or say harsh words because you're disappointed or feel hurt. Instead, depart with grace and dignity. Such an attitude will help preserve the relationships you worked so hard to cultivate. You will need favorable references to help you obtain a new job, and the most important references are those from your previous employer.

Core Strategy for Success

Of course, networking is of little value unless you have the knowledge and skills necessary to succeed in your dream job. As previously stressed, having a passion for learning (the "L" in the ECL Core Strategy for Success) is the critical driver that helps you prepare for future opportunities and then be successful when they do occur.

To sum it up, the best overall advice to find your dream job and keep it is to: 1) develop expertise in a needed area, 2) be a top-notch performer, and 3) network extensively.

Chapter Twenty-Four

What if You Dislike Your Job?

"No one keeps up his enthusiasm automatically. Enthusiasm must be nourished with new actions, new aspirations, new efforts, and new vision. It is one's fault if his enthusiasm is gone; he has failed to feed it."

—Papyrus

Although it may not be possible for everyone to secure his or her dream job, it's certainly worth pursuing. But what if you're stuck in a job that you dislike and are having difficulty finding one you'd really enjoy? If this happens, you essentially have two choices. The first one is to keep working where you are and continue having negative thoughts about how horrible your situation is.

If you elect this approach, it will be only a matter of time until your negative attitude is recognized by your peers and eventually by senior management. No matter how well you perform, no one will put up for long with an individual who constantly complains and infects associates with negativism. There are just too many other good people with positive attitudes available in the marketplace.

Your second choice is to keep working where you are, but change your mind set about it until something better comes along. As the well-known nineteenth century psychologist and philosopher William James said, "The greatest discovery of my generation is that a human being can alter his life by altering his attitude of mind." In his book, *The Fred Factor*, Mark Sanborn adds, "The person doing the work determines the difference between the mundane and the magnificent."

> *... when we work for others, our efforts return to bless us.*
>
> **Sidney Powell**
> (Author)

Take the old story of the three men hauling stones in wheelbarrows at a construction site. A stranger approaches them and asks each man what he's doing. The first one replies, "I'm hauling rocks." The second man says, "I'm helping build a wall." The third man responds, "I'm building a cathedral." If you were an employer, which man would you hire? The obvious answer is the third one because he's proud of what he's doing and the extent of work pride is an excellent predictor of performance.

According to Tal Ben-Shahar, PhD, "In a study of hospital janitors, one group experienced their work as boring and meaningless, but the other group perceived the same work as engaging and meaningful because they crafted their duties in creative ways."[43] He continues by saying, "The second group interacted more with nurses and patients, and they saw their work not merely as removing the garbage and dirty linen, but contributing to the patients' well-being and the smooth functioning of the hospital."[44]

The bottom line is that even though you may not be ecstatic about your present job, try to view it as contributing to the welfare of the customers who use your products or services.

Focus on how you are making life fuller and richer for them. If you adopt this kind of service attitude, it will not be long until you're recognized for your good work, which, in turn, will lead to job opportunities that might be more rewarding and enjoyable.

Finally, while stuck in a job you dislike, don't waste a lot of emotional energy feeling sorry for yourself. Such a "woe-is-me" attitude is debilitating. Instead, decide to apply your energy in a positive manner by developing the expertise necessary for success in your preferred career field. This involves utilizing the principles of continuous self-development outlined in the previous chapters.

> *Don't wait for your situation to change before you put your heart into your work . . . bloom where you are planted.*
>
> **Charles Swindoll**
> (Author and educator)

In summary, "Z" stands for zeal—having the determination to live an ethical life, to have a "caring for others" spirit, and to be a lifelong learner. In addition, it stands for having enthusiasm for your work. All of the above are critical for long-term leadership success.

Chapter Twenty-Five

"Z" Strategy Takeaways

1. The attitude of zeal is necessary to make the ECL Core Strategy for Success work for you. It's also important to have zeal for one's work.
2. When people are zealous about their work, they give their heart and soul to it. This gives them a tremendous advantage over others who lack enthusiasm for what they do.
3. People who have zeal for their work have positive attitudes, are extremely focused, and do more than what is required of them.
4. Seek work that you truly enjoy.
5. The best way to find your dream job is to: a) establish a strong performance reputation and b) network extensively by steadily increasing the number and quality of your business and social contacts.
6. Personal contacts are the best source of job opportunities.
7. Never "burn your bridges" when you leave an employer.
8. If you truly dislike your present job, continue the quest for one that you would enjoy. Meanwhile, do

the best you can where you are by adopting a service attitude toward your associates and customers. This means viewing what you do as contributing to their welfare. Above all, try to focus outwardly on others rather than on yourself. In addition, use your spare time to develop the expertise necessary for a career in a field you would enjoy.

Section Seven

Postscript on Successful Living

The great concept about America is that no matter what your race, gender, or religion, you can strive to become just about anything you want in life. You can aspire to be the CEO of a large company, a business owner, a member of Congress, or even the President of the United States. Obtaining such levels are certainly strong measurements of one's success. But to me, what is really important in measuring success is not how much wealth, power, and fame you acquire, but rather how you live your life as measured by the following criteria:

- Your ethics—the type of positive example you set for others in terms of doing what is right, good, honest, and fair.

> *True success is best measured by how you use the precious gift of your life. You have the power to either waste it or make it meaningful.*

- The extent to which you have a "caring for others" spirit.
- Your determination to continually develop yourself in order to reach your highest leadership potential.

If you always try to do your very best to live by ECL, you will be successful in life.

The point is that you were created with the potential to make a positive difference in this world. The fulfillment of this blessing is totally up to you!

Let's face it, when your time on Earth is done, the thousands of people you came in contact with throughout the years will not remember your significant achievements at work and in public service, neither will they care about how much money you made. Rather, they will recall the nature of your character and how it had a positive influence on them. In addition, people will remember with fondness the kind things you did for them in their time of need. The same is true for your children and grandchildren. What will stick in their minds throughout their lives will be the details of the intimate love you gave them, the good times you shared with them, and the positive things you did to develop and support them.

Dr. Norman Vincent Peale said, "The person who lives for himself or herself is a failure; the person who lives for others has achieved true success." Actor and philanthropist Danny Thomas said it another way: "Success in life has nothing to do with what you gain or accomplish for yourself; it's what you do for others."

Section Eight

Summary:
How to Lead the Pack

Live a life that makes a difference!

In summary, the possibility of achieving your highest potential as a leader is considerably enhanced if you adopt and continually practice ECL.

- "E" for Ethics
- "C" for Caring for others
- "L" for Lifelong learning

When these three key leadership values are put together in the format of a simple formula, this is the result:

ECL Core Strategy for Success:

**E (Ethics) + C (Caring for Others) = inspired employees
+ L (Lifelong Learning) = long-term success**

Core Strategy for Success

The Core Strategy for Success enables something even more important than the traditional measurements of success (e.g., money, status, and power). It provides the opportunity for a person to live a life that is joy-filled and meaningful— meaningful in the sense that it makes a difference in the lives of others!

Section Nine

References

[1] "The Josephson Institute of Ethics Releases Study on High School Character and Adult conduct," www.josephsoninstitute.org, October 29, 2009.

[2] Bob Herbert, "A Sin and a Shame," *New York Times On-line Digest,* July 31, 2010.

[3] Ibid.

[4] "CEOs Claim Jackpots Amid Layoffs," *Island Packet,* September 15, 2010, p. 8A.

[5] "A Change of Heart for College Students," *USA Today,* June 8, 2010.

[6] "Americans Look for a Return to Values," *Investor Business Daily,* November 29, 2010.

[7] Ferrell, Fraedrich, and Ferrell, *Business Ethics,* (Mason, Ohio: South-Western Cengage Learning, 2010), p. 8.

[8] Robert S. Wieder, "Dr. Truth," *Success Magazine*

[9] Ibid.

[10] Remi Trudel and June Cotte, "Does Being Ethical Pay?" *Wall Street Journal,* May 12, 2008.

Core Strategy for Success

[11] Whole Foods, Inc. brochure titled "Whole Trade Guarantee."

[12] "A Study of the Link between a Corporation's Financial Performance and Its Commitment to Ethics," *Journal of Business Ethics,* October, 1998, p. 1,509.

[13] Jack Canfield and Mark Victor Hansen, *A 2nd Helping of Chicken Soup for the Soul* (Deerfield Beach: Health Communications, 1995), p. 36.

[14] Ken Blanchard and Dr. Norman Vincent Peale, *The Power of Ethical Management.*

[15] Ken Blanchard, *The Heart of the Leader* (Tulsa: Honor Books, 1999), p. 27.

[16] Joanne B. Ciulla, *Ethics: The Heart of Leadership* (Westport: Praeger Publishers, 1998), p. 29.

[17] John Maxwell, *Ethics 101* (New York: Center Street, 2003), p. 18.

[18] "CEO's Moral Compass Steers Siemens," *USA Today,* February 15, 2010, p. 3B.

[19] Ibid.

[20] *Lasting Leadership—What You Can Learn from the Top 25 Business People of Our Times* (Upper Saddle River: Wharton School of Publishing, 2005), p.10.

[21] Ken Blanchard and Phil Hodges, *Lead Like Jesus, Lessons from the Greatest Leadership Role Model of all Time* (New York: Thomas Nelson, 2005), p.40.

[22] Gail Sheehy, "The Secret to Longer Life May Surprise You," *USA Today,* November 30, 2010.

[23] Gary Smith, "Someone to Lean On," *Sports Illustrated,* December 16, 1996.

[24] David Lauderdale, "Radio Kennedy Helps Us Tune into the Joys of Life," *Island Packet,* April 19, 2009.

[25] *USA Today,* January 4, 2007.

[26] Ibid.

[27] Robert Cooper, PhD, *Emotional Intelligence in Leadership and Organizations* (New York: Ayman Sawaf Berkley Publishing Co., 1997), p. 204.

[28] Jack Canfield and Mark Victor Hansen, *Chicken Soup for the Soul: 101Stories to Open the Heart and Rekindle the Spirit* (Deerfield Beach: 1993), p.278.

[29] Joseph Nocera, "Living with Layoffs," *Fortune,* April 1, 1996.

[30] Nicholas. Varchaver, "What Warren Thinks," *Fortune,* April 28, 2008.

[31] Brent Schlender, "Gates after Microsoft," *Fortune,* July 7, 2008, p.110.

[32] *Fortune,* May 14, 2007.

[33] Ibid.

[34] Warren Bennis and Bert Nanus, *Leaders* (New York: Harper and Row Publishers, 1995), p. 188.

[35] Ibid.

[36] "What Would You Do With an Extra Hour?" *Wall Street Journal,* June 23, 2010.

[37] Anne Fisher, "What's the One Piece of Advice You Had Been Given?" *Fortune,* June 23, 2003, p.142.

[38] David Aikman, *Great Souls: Six Who Changed the Century,* (Nashville: Word Publishing, 1998).

[39] Ibid.

[40] Bennis and Nanus, *Leaders,* p.70.

[41] Ibid.

[42] "Take Control of Your Career," *Fortune,* November 18, 1991, p. 92

[43] Tal Ben-Shahar, PhD, *101 Anti-aging Secrets,* (New York: Board Room, Inc. 2008).

[44] Ibid.